PITTSBURGH
AND THE
GREAT STEEL STRIKE
OF 1919

PITTSBURGH
AND THE
GREAT STEEL STRIKE
of **1919**

RYAN C. BROWN

THE
History
PRESS

Published by The History Press
Charleston, SC
www.historypress.com

First published 2019

Manufactured in the United States

ISBN 9781467142588

Library of Congress Control Number: 2019943512

Notice: The information in this book is true and complete to the best of our knowledge. It is offered without guarantee on the part of the author or The History Press. The author and The History Press disclaim all liability in connection with the use of this book.

To Kelly

CONTENTS

ACKNOWLEDGEMENTS

Nothing of value is built solely by its immediate creator. The great libraries and museums that bear the names of steel moguls could only be built through the work of the mills, just as the millworkers relied on ore and coal miners, railroad workers and thousands of unsung wives and mothers.

Similarly, this book isn't the sole work of its author; many family members, friends, teachers and advisors helped along the way, and each lent their own labor and value to the final product.

This book couldn't be in your hands without the editors and artists at The History Press who aided me at every step.

I would like to thank my wife, Kelly, whose encouragement and patience made this project possible. I would also like to thank my mother, Laura; my father, Chris; my stepfather, Dustin; my stepmother, Brenda; and my wife's parents, Greg and Cheryl, who all contributed time and energy to make our lives easier while I researched and wrote this book. I want to thank my brother, Simon, who offered advice as a historian, and my grandparents Herbert and Shirley Brankley—both are Pittsburgh natives who raised a family there and provided inspiration for this book.

I owe thanks to my former newspaper coworkers and editors, whose advice helped sharpen my writing, and to Lee Wood, whose tough journalism lessons hopefully helped keep this book clear and concise. I would also like to thank Jared Frederick of Penn State Altoona, a friend and talented historian who encouraged me to begin this project.

This book would not have been possible without the aid of researchers, particularly those who maintain archives and online repositories to little fanfare. I extend my thanks to the archivists at the University of Pittsburgh, the Historic Pittsburgh collections and to Tim Davenport, whose online collection of American Marxist history was of great help.

While I relied on the work of many great authors, researchers and journalists, a special thanks is owed to Charles H. McCormick, whose book *Seeing Reds* was of singular importance.

I thank those around Pittsburgh who have worked to preserve the city's industrial and labor heritage. Groups like the Battle of Homestead Foundation have been an invaluable resource.

Lastly, I thank the many union members, labor activists and organizers whom I have had the honor to meet and work with. Their perspectives on today's conflicts helped me understand the labor battles of a century past.

INTRODUCTION

From the steps of the Good Shepherd Catholic Parish in Braddock, Pennsylvania, there are two buildings that catch the eye. First, just a few yards away across Braddock Avenue, is the office of the United Steelworkers Local 1219. Behind it, looming over the city like a rusty blue ship, is the Edgar Thomson Plant of the United States Steel Corporation.

The plant stretches along the Monongahela River and is crisscrossed by railroad tracks and power lines. It can churn out millions of tons of steel each year that is shipped to other U.S. Steel facilities that still dot the Pennsylvania valleys. It has stood there, in one form or another, since the 1870s, when the plant's Bessemer converter first poured out its purified steel. The monstrous ladles and chargers have been modernized, but still, the plant makes steel.

It's easy to miss the office of Local 1219 in the mill's shadow. The low-slung building is host to occasional union meetings and Steelers viewing parties, and a few cars can usually be found parked along Eleventh Street. A visitor might find it hard to imagine the scene that was on that street in October 1919: crowds of men openly battling outside the mill, replacement workers fighting their way inside under police guard, a state constable wounded in the mêlée, a man shot—it's not clear who, which was often the case in the chaotic and garbled reports that flowed from the battles in every steel town. The *Pittsburgh Gazette Times* could only report that Washington Street was "the scene of other troubles between strike sympathizers and workmen during the day."

There was no union hall then. The workers, who spent twelve-hour days and seven-day weeks in the blazing mill, had no union, at least not a recognized one. Those who joined risked dismissal, the blacklist and beatings by industrial agents. An unprecedented organizing drive had spurred thousands of workers around Pittsburgh to join the Amalgamated Association of Iron and Steel Workers, which sought a raft of reforms and recognition to bargain as equals with the millionaire steel bosses. However, it was nothing like today's organizing drives. From the 1930s until the modern wave of so-called right-to-work legislation, workers and employers in the United States dealt on the principle that a fairly elected union represented all the employees under its jurisdiction. But in 1919, the steel bosses were under no obligation to make a deal. They fought the organizers, and their supporters, with government support.

For months, the valleys around Pittsburgh—the Monongahela, the Allegheny, the Ohio, the Shenango, the Conemaugh and many more—were in an effective state of war. Sheriffs deputized thousands of civilians and handed enforcement of the law over to eager, anti-union men and soldiers fresh from the trenches of World War I in France. Strikers armed themselves and surrounded the mills, desperate to keep replacements from relighting the furnaces. Many died—twenty according to organizers—but figures vary. At the time, it was the largest strike in America.

There was a church in Braddock's battlefield, too, but the Good Shepherd Parish had not yet been built. Its predecessor, St. Michael's Parish, rang with the songs of Slovak immigrants who had crossed an ocean to work in the mills. The workers had crossed from the Austro-Hungarian Empire, and their families often followed. Along with them were thousands of poor immigrants from the new and old nations of Europe: Russia, Poland, Romania and Croatia. Those immigrants were at the heart of the strike, and at St. Michael's, the parish priest tended to their hungry families and stood with their union. When the authorities threatened the church, the priest vowed to fly a banner atop the steeple to place blame on the steel bosses.

The immigrants also brought with them new ideas from Europe, which terrified steel moguls, newspapermen and politicians alike. Across Pittsburgh and its surrounding towns, socialist meeting halls and schools sprung up. Parties and unions with strange names formed, and their meetings were sometimes carried out in strange languages. "Lenin" and "Trotsky" became household names in America. Among Pittsburgh's immigrants—and its natural-born citizens—groups like the Communist Labor Party, the Union of Russian Workers and the Industrial Workers of the World drew newfound attention. "Why work for wages?" they asked. They said that system that allowed steel moguls to live in sprawling mountain castles while condemning steelworkers to shantytowns couldn't last. A general strike, a workers' uprising, could end it.

This was Pittsburgh in 1918, 1919 and 1920, the years when America seemed on the verge of a revolution. A century later, those days would appear almost unrecognizable. The city's once-great radical gathering halls have been demolished or turned into bars and attorneys' offices. Many of the old steel mills have been shut down or operate with a fraction of the workforce they once employed. But signs of this turbulent time remain everywhere if you know where to look. And the spirit of 1919 remains, too; steelworkers still gather in their union halls, U.S. Steel executives still meet in a skyscraper towering over the city.

In 2018, a wave of strikes roared across the country, led, in several states, by teachers who, in some cases, walked off of their jobs illegally. In Pittsburgh and cities across the country, meeting halls were once again filled with labor and left-wing radicals of every stripe; "socialism" entered the common political parlance for the first time in decades. This organization of U.S. workers would, in no doubt, shock Elbert Gary, who headed U.S. Steel and demanded an "open shop," and hearten William Z. Foster, who organized the steelworkers from his Pittsburgh office.

The lessons of the Great Steel Strike of 1919 remain important a century later, and so do its physical scars, for those willing to look for them.

1

TWO DEATHS

August 11, 1919

From Massachusetts and New York, the news traveled almost instantaneously over the Alleghenies and into Pittsburgh newsrooms. Updates poured in by wire; editors pieced together towering headlines and spread obituaries across several pages.

Within hours, the first papers appeared on the city's streets:

"ANDREW CARNEGIE DEAD."

Statesmen, power-brokers and industrial millionaires all paid tribute to the tycoon who had died at eighty-three years old after a brief bout of pneumonia. The *Pittsburgh Gazette-Times* reported, "Immediately, the news of Mr. Carnegie's death was flashed to the world, messages of condolence from great men of affairs all over the country began to arrive." Charles M. Schwab, head of Bethlehem Steel, called Carnegie "the greatest man I ever knew."

When the news arrived in Pittsburgh, it struck the empire that had been built in Carnegie's name. Readers learned of his death in the shadow of the Carnegie Building downtown, on the campus of the Carnegie Institute of Technology and in the borough of Carnegie along Chartiers Creek. Reports on his death would appear in the dozens of Carnegie libraries across Pennsylvania, which had each been donated from the millionaire's seemingly endless pool of wealth. W.J. Holland, former chancellor of the University of Pittsburgh and director of the Carnegie Museum, eulogized him:

> *A continent was being opened up to human occupation. There were railways to be built, great streams required to be bridged, towns and cities were called into being. He was at the center of the movement, in close touch with quiet but forceful men, who were the leaders. He dwelt in the midst of opportunities. He recognized them as they arose and embraced them. One door quickly opened and then another, and he pressed on, laughing as he went. At last he said to himself, "I have had enough of this!"*

Mourners said Carnegie's life read like a romance, and indeed it did. Born in a Scottish weaver's cottage, he moved with his family to the United States as a boy and soon found work on the railroads. The young Carnegie was made superintendent of the Pennsylvania Railroad's western branch, where he made enough money to invest in businesses of his own. At the height of the Civil War, with Northern industry churning out arms and ammunition for millions of men, no business was riper for investment than ironmaking.

Sitting among coal-rich hills and tied into the country's greatest waterways, the young city of Pittsburgh was perfectly set for the rise of steel. The revolution that began in England a century earlier had exploded around the world and enveloped distant colonies, where whole countries of farmers became industrial armies. The rise of global industry required tools, ships and, above all, railroads. After the Civil War, a network of railways appeared across the United States, drawing cities together and directly connecting the East and West Coasts for the first time. In one generation, from 1840 to 1870, rail lines expanded from a few East Coast stretches totaling less than three thousand miles to a nationwide web that totaled fifty thousand miles. Entire cities sprung up along railroads: Chicago went from a small town of a few thousand residents to a sprawling metropolis of nearly three hundred thousand.

All of this development required iron and steel in tremendous quantities. In their early days, Pennsylvania iron furnaces were small-scale, individual businesses, which often ran in small towns or remote areas with largely manual labor forces. The stages of production—from raw iron ore to finished rails, wheels or steamboat parts—were often separated by distance and ownership.

The process was complex. First, ironmakers obtained iron ore that was mined, initially, from small, scattered veins. The ore was then transported to

Andrew Carnegie, founder
of Carnegie Steel Co.
Library of Congress.

furnaces where skilled workers would reduce it to a finished product. This process required additional materials, including a fuel capable of raising the ore to a high enough temperature that a blast of heated air could separate the iron from the unwanted, extraneous material. Mills also needed a flux material to help pull the waste product, called slag, from the purified iron. Workers labored alongside blazing fires and sparking molten iron in this early process, since there was no automation available to replace skill and experience. Some elements of the job were little changed from medieval times, including the use of charcoal as a fuel. This made the work slow and labor-intensive, and the final product was too brittle for many uses.

Methods to improve the finished product were equally labor-intensive, and often deadly. In the mid-nineteenth century, so-called puddlers were the men responsible for making stronger bar iron from the comparatively weak pig iron that poured, glowing hot, from steel furnaces. Puddlers loaded iron into vats where hot gas passed over the iron's surface until it formed a molten, bubbling mass. They then stirred the material with long iron bars—which would also gradually melt into the mix—and painstakingly formed the resulting balls of iron into long, tough bars suitable for construction. "They are subjected to a constant bombardment of sparks, and must wear masks to protect their faces," an observer would later note. "They are obliged also to stand on steel plates, hot from the iron that is always passing over them. The roll hands wear shoes with heavy wooden soles, but in spite of these their feet are always hot."

Pittsburgh's first successful blast furnace, the Clinton Furnace, was built in 1859 on the South Side as part of a new wave of efficient, vertically integrated producers. Built by investors who already owned a rolling mill that created the finished iron product, the furnace used coke from the rich Connellsville range instead of antiquated charcoal. Coke was produced by reducing coal over several days in round, beehive-shaped furnaces, and it was a high-grade fuel perfect for producing iron. The foul coke production process belched fumes and smoke into the air and left piles of coal slag alongside industrial towns.

The Clinton Furnace quickly set production records by blasting impurities from the ore at a far higher pressure than its competitors. More furnaces followed, and within two decades, Pittsburgh was the country's most prominent iron-producing district. It was during this period that Carnegie first made his mark on the industry and gained a reputation for ruthless efficiency and constant expansion.

Carnegie followed his Keystone Bridge Co. with an 1870 venture alongside his brother, Thomas, to build the Lucy and Isabella Furnaces along the Allegheny River. The seventy-five-foot-tall furnaces towered over their surroundings and dwarfed the Clinton Furnace. Both furnaces produced tens of thousands of tons of iron each year, and when one of the twin plants reported producing one hundred tons in a single day, it "was heard with incredulity in the iron trade," newspapers later reported.

It was from Europe that Carnegie first adopted the Bessemer process, the system of steel production that would revolutionize the industry. By the early 1870s, railroads were expanding at a breakneck pace, and strong steel was needed in once-unimaginable quantities. Carnegie, his investors and an army of workers provided it along with the Edgar Thomson Works in Braddock. A tiny paragraph in the August 28, 1875 edition of the *Pittsburgh Daily Post* notified readers that "the first heat of steel was made at the J. Edgar Thomson Steel Works" and noted that "only a few gentlemen were present." But the event—coupled with the adoption of the Bessemer technique at other Pittsburgh furnaces—would inaugurate a new era of automation and productivity. In the production of steel, finished iron was loaded into a

The Lucy Furnace, Andrew Carnegie's first iron project in Pittsburgh. The mill's productivity surged past competitors, launching the city's steel trade. *Library of Congress.*

towering, egg-shaped vat, which was then turned upward to force charged air into the molten metal. The blast removed impurities in the iron, which workers would then empty into a channel below in the form of molten steel. Iron turned into Bessemer steel in as little as ten minutes, versus as much as a day using older methods.

Skilled supervisors led the work and gauged by eye when the steel was ready to pour. Guessing incorrectly meant wasted work and lost money, and bosses like Carnegie, who had built their careers as foremen and supervisors, established tough systems to enforce efficiency. "When operating them, a careful record was kept of the costs. You are expected always to get it ten cents cheaper the next year or the next month," a former Carnegie manager later said before a congressional committee. "The pressure is always on to make all the economies you can."

Carnegie's facilities were far from the only ones operating in this kind of environment. Jones and Laughlin Steel Co. switched from iron to steel in the 1880s, and the Cambria Iron Co., later the Cambria Steel Co., offered competition in the bituminous coal country of Johnstown. An array of competing producers and innovations in technology placed downward pressure on steel prices as managers strained to control costs and keep an edge in profits. This was the age of Taylorism, the system of scientific management that sought to rationalize workflows even if the workers themselves suffered for it. "The principle at Pittsburgh was to destroy anything from a steam hammer to a steel works whenever a better piece of apparatus was to be had," said a contemporary industrial writer. "Thousands of dollars are spent to dispense with the labor of one or two men."

Carnegie benefited tremendously from the industry's growth. One by one, he took control of competing furnaces and established his own until he eventually merged them into a colossal company based in a fifteen-story skyscraper along Fifth Avenue. By 1889, with the United States outproducing Britain in steel, he outlined his philosophy on wealth in the *North American Review* magazine:

> *While the law* [of competition] *may be sometimes hard for the individual, it is best for the race, because it insures the survival of the fittest in every department. We accept and welcome, therefore, as conditions to which we must accommodate ourselves, great inequality of environment, the concentration of business, industrial and commercial, in the hands of the few, and the law of competition between these, as being not only beneficial, but essential for the future progress of the race.*

The steel bosses held the power of life and death over those who worked in their mills and lived in the towns surrounding them. In 1889, the South Fork Dam, which had been altered to suit the needs of a wealthy hunting and fishing club whose members included Carnegie and his lieutenants, burst open, leaving a wall of water to annihilate Johnstown and kill more than 2,200 people. Carnegie would fund one of his trademark libraries in Johnstown soon afterward.

Even early labor struggles, which foreshadowed the mass organizations and violent strikes that would follow, quickly ended in the steelmen's favor. In 1892, laborers at Carnegie's Homestead Works struck and seized control of their town. Henry Clay Frick, Carnegie's ally and second-in-command, ordered armed strikebreakers to ruthlessly end the revolt. The resulting battle was a pyrrhic victory for the workers, who were locked out, dispersed with government force and replaced by non-union laborers in a lasting blow to the movement. The steel owners' power was unquestionable, and they

The aftermath of the 1889 flood in Johnstown. A lake, dammed by steel magnates and their associates for fishing and recreation, burst into the city and killed thousands. *Library of Congress.*

held a firm grip over local governments and lawmakers. The Coal and Iron Police, a state-controlled force funded and employed by bosses to put down strikes, would soon be joined by the Pennsylvania State Police force, which quickly went to work battling strikers and ensuring peace at the mills.

Looking back, it seems inevitable that the steel giants would merge their power and end the competition that held back their profits. No matter what Carnegie thought of "the law of competition," investors could see the benefit of a grand steel trust, one that would be in control of more than half the nation's productive capacity. By early 1901, Pittsburgh newspapers buzzed with rumors. The great financier J.P. Morgan planned to absorb several huge steel companies, including Carnegie's, and end the age of competition in steel. "It is probable there will be such ownership and control as to secure perfect and permanent harmony in the larger lines of this industry," the *Pittsburgh Post* wrote, citing representatives of Morgan's project. Weeks later, Morgan formally established U.S. Steel, combining Carnegie's company with a series of smaller steel producers with names like Federal Steel, National Tube and American Tin Plate. Run from New York, the new company set prices and dealt with organized labor as a united front.

The new company would also make Carnegie incredibly rich. When Charles Schwab asked what it would take to obtain the country's most powerful steel company, the sixty-five-year-old Carnegie slipped him a piece of paper with a written figure: $480 million. This fortune was enough to make the Scottish immigrant the world's most renowned philanthropist; he showered money on a number of causes from the arts and libraries to anti-imperialism efforts in the Philippines. When his successors at U.S. Steel touted a new plan to offer workers stock in the company, the retired Carnegie—ever in favor of gifts and benefits, even if workers remained unorganized—praised it as a solution to the eternal battle between "capital and labor."

Carnegie retained a personal interest in the empire he had created in the city of Pittsburgh, where so many buildings and public works bear his name. The forges he funded and oversaw, from Lucy along the Allegheny to the sprawling Edgar Thomson Works, still towered over the city and its surrounding towns. Mary Heaton Vorse, a British journalist who would later tour the region while covering its labor battles, described "the Principality of Steel" Carnegie had helped create:

> The industry has progressed mightily. There is no prouder achievement in American industry than steel—in manufacture of steel, we surpass the world. Sheffield is an old man in his dotage. Newcastle sleeps. Pittsburgh is to-day making to-morrow....In the steel towns they make the raw materials for all the swift moving things; the wheels of great machines, the engines which move trains and vessels and airships, the frame-work of high buildings. Our civilization is forged in the steel towns.

Carnegie spent his final days at his sprawling, castle-like estate at Shadow Brook in the Berkshires of western Massachusetts. He spent hours each day in his flower garden, newspapers reported, and he enjoyed fishing trips at the lake on his electric motorboat. "He loved all kinds of flowers, especially pungent verbena and heliotrope and many kinds of wild flowers," the *Pittsburgh Gazette Times* noted a day after his death. "He wore nearly every day a sprig of verbena in the buttonhole of his homespun sack coat."

Carnegie passed away in his castle, a doctor at the bedside and his flowers growing outside. In the Principality of Steel, however, death did not always come so peacefully.

August 26, 1919

Fannie Sellins was holding her post on the picket line. Flanked by miners of the Allegheny Coal and Coke Co., the widow and grandmother faced down county sheriff's deputies who, according to union men, had promised to "make it rough for the miners."

As a woman in her fifties, Sellins was an experienced organizer for the United Mine Workers of America. She had organized garment workers in St. Louis and miners in West Virginia, but in the years leading up to 1919, she had dedicated her efforts to the coal mines of the Pittsburgh steel district. It wasn't an easy task; in parts of the Allegheny-Kiski valleys where steel companies operated "captive" mines, workers had proven resistant to unions. Despite this, Sellins was able to succeed, and she even organized southern black workers who had been brought in to break strikes and replace union men. Strikes began to break out periodically in coal country, and organizers and bosses began fighting a hit-and-run battle over new "scab" crews that had been hauled in to take over the mines.

The Allegheny Coal and Coke bosses were fed up with the union in Brackenridge, union organizers wrote. The strike had remained peaceful, but on the morning of August 26, deputies warned the miners: they were armed, and the miners could expect a fight. Shouts and jeers were exchanged, a scuffle began and then a flurry of gunshots rang out.

When the scene cleared, Sellins was lying dead along with Joseph Strzelcki, a fifty-four-year-old miner. A coroner's report revealed the details; someone had fired two shots into Sellins's head, which pierced her skull and caused death by hemorrhage. The gunman shot Strzelcki five times in the abdomen and left him to bleed to death on the ground outside of the mine. Several others were wounded, and at least one was struck in the head with a club or mace. Investigators named two suspects—sheriff's deputies who claimed self-defense—but union officials expressed little hope for a fair punishment. The Pittsburgh Central Labor Union, which claimed to represent 180,000 workers, called it "the most atrocious and cruel double murder ever committed in Allegheny County." They said, "There have been two brutal murders committed at West Natrona....All the evidence adduced to date shows plainly that said murders were committed

Mounted state constables stand guard during a strike in McKees Rocks. *Library of Congress.*

by deputies in employ of the sheriff's office....These murders have all the signs of being planned beforehand, and as a result, being premeditated."

Throughout the coal and steel communities, Sellins's name became a battle cry. When Vorse, the British journalist covering the labor unrest, watched a meeting of union men in Youngstown, the pent-up rage was palpable. An excited crowd of "wide-shouldered, strong-looking" steelworkers—Poles, Slovaks, Croats, Italians, Romanians and African Americans—packed themselves into a meeting hall to discuss their efforts.

> *Their mood changed. It was as though clouds had darkened the sky. Their faces became hard. The faces of the crowd mirrored their anger as the sea mirrors an approaching storm. I heard the name Fanny Sellins. The organizer was speaking earnestly, without gesture, bent over slightly from the hips, talking down into the faces of the crowd. "Fanny Sellins" and again "Fanny Sellins" I heard him repeat, while the face of the crowd darkened and grew still with silent menace.*

The Allegheny County coroner's investigators saw a different menace. The officials claimed in a formal report that the crowd of strikers "threw stones, bottles and sticks of wood at the deputys [*sic*]" and refused to disperse. A month after Sellins's and Strzelcki's deaths, a jury impaneled by the county coroner rendered its verdict. It wasn't out-of-control deputies who caused their deaths—it was a dangerous new ideology.

The jury find death was…justifiable and in self-defense and also recommend that Sheriff Haddock be commended in his prompt and successful action in protecting property and persons in that vicinity, and the judgment exercised in the selection of his deputies. We also criticize and deplore the action of alien or agitators who instill anarchy and Bolshevism doctrines in the minds of un-Americans and uneducated aliens.

Today, a monument to Sellins and Strzelcki stands over Union Cemetery in Arnold, Westmoreland County. Under the old emblem of the United Mine Workers is an inscription: "Nobly you fought the fight against greed and gain / Never Flinching with your efforts when the bullets came / Immortal to the miners shall ever be thy name / Embellished in their hearts the sacrifice you made."

LIFE AMONG THE MILLS

The "un-American and uneducated aliens" who made up Pittsburgh's industrial armies still drew distrust, even hatred, long after they had first arrived in the steel towns. By the eve of World War I, some eighty thousand steelworkers lived in Allegheny County, from unskilled laborers to highly trained foremen. The makeup of the community had changed completely in just a few years. What had once been a population of American-born, British and German workers had become supplanted by a force of eastern European immigrants. Hailing from the Russian Empire and the Habsburg kingdoms of Austria-Hungary, these immigrants' ethnic differences confused census-takers and gave their American-born colleagues opportunities to dismiss them all as "hunkies." Many immigrants did not expect to stay in America for the rest of their lives, and indeed, many did not; once they had saved enough of their wages, some returned to their families in Croatia, Poland or Bohemia to buy new farms and houses.

Census forms demonstrate this demographic shift in Monongahela Valley steel towns. By 1910, entire pages list "Slovak" and "Italian" from top to bottom, and many lived in packed rental houses where poorly paid

An unidentified mill street in Pittsburgh around the turn of the twentieth century. Life revolved around the mills, with workers covering twelve-hour shifts every day. *Library of Congress.*

immigrant workers shared beds in shifts. In 1907, more than 55 percent of the Carnegie plants' workforce was listed as "Slavic" in ethnicity—used as a general term for eastern European immigrants—as compared to the 25 percent of workers listed as American-born. Irish-born workers, who, just a generation earlier, had composed a huge share of the steel armies, now represented just 6 percent of the workforce. A sort of ethnic hierarchy was enforced at the steel mills, based partly in time served and partly in xenophobia and a sense of superiority. Many so-called white workers refused to take work assigned to Slavic immigrants, and some even took worse or lower-paying jobs as long as they came with a sense of social superiority—the ability to wear office clothes instead of overalls, for example. John Griswold, a Scotch-Irish furnace boss, described how the long hours and work conditions drove Irishmen out of the mills and left them to be replaced by "furriners":

> *It ain't the Hunkies—they couldn't do it—but the Irish don't have to work this way. There was fifty of them here with me sixteen years ago and now where are they? I meet 'em sometimes around the city, ridin' in carriages and all of them wearin' white shirts, and here I am with these Hunkies. They don't seem like men to me hardly. They can't talk United States. You tell them something and they just look and say, "Me no fustay, me no fustay," and that's all you can get out of 'em. And here I am with them all the time, twelve hours a day and every day and I'm all alone—not a mother's son of 'em that I can talk to.*

Hiring bosses sought out new immigrants, and some would contract with more experienced and savvy foreign workers in order to hire them in groups. The less scrupulous of these hiring bosses took cash from new arrivals seeking work. A *Pittsburgh Gazette Times* "work wanted" ad from 1909 seeks tinners, catchers and helpers for "steady employment and good wages" but notes that "Syrians, Poles and Romanians" are preferred. In industrial towns and cities across the country, immigrants were seen as expendable. The *Pittsburgh Gazette Times* implored its readers to see beyond ethnicity when it said in 1913, "The chances are one hundred to one that the average person who read last week in the Pittsburgh papers of the death by drowning of Michael Demjanovic, aged sixteen, dismissed the item with a mental comment 'only a Hunky.'" Slavic and Italian immigrants were rarely, if ever, promoted to higher jobs, and during economic downturns, American-born applicants would be hired in their place.

The work they did was brutal and often dangerous. Between 1906 and 1907, 195 steelworkers in the Pittsburgh district died in plants, according to a study at the time by progressive investigator John A. Fitch. The causes of death were horrifying: 22 died in hot metal explosions, 24 died from high falls into pits and 5 died from "asphyxiation by furnace gas." In 1907, a furnace owned by the Jones and Laughlin company exploded and instantly burned 14 men to death.

The work in the furnaces had changed tremendously since the Clinton Furnace poured out its first river of hot iron. Most of the eighty thousand workers in the Pittsburgh district were considered unskilled as a result of Carnegie and his colleagues' constant drive for automation and efficiency. Where workers had once hand-loaded iron into steel furnaces and stood atop the boiling mass, electric skips now dumped the material with the pull of a lever. Where puddlers had once spent hours stirring iron bars into a molten concoction and relied on an experienced eye to know when the product was ready, workers now loaded their material into massive open hearths and used scientific measurements to meet the precise strength requirements of railroads and shipbuilders. As in nearly every industry, work once restricted

The Jones and Laughlin Steel Works at the turn of the twentieth century. Sprawling mills lined the Monongahela River. *Library of Congress.*

to trained craftsmen was now available to armies of regimented workers who were all considered replaceable. Workers were usually capable of performing the task above their own, Fitch noted, and when one moved up, quit or died, another could simply be slotted into his place.

The transformation of Pittsburgh's steel industry did not lead to an improvement in conditions for its workers. Almost every worker had twelve-hour days, and many had to work occasional twenty-four-hour shifts to cover night turns. Nineteenth-century puddlers had spent much of their shifts watching and waiting, and when two shifts finished their iron bars, they could close for the night. This was not so in the twentieth-century mills of U.S. Steel, Bethlehem and Jones and Laughlin. Leaving a steel furnace to cool meant possible damage, and a lost night shift meant lost revenue. Work continued through every Sunday, and most workers put in somewhere between seventy-two and eighty-four hours per week. The number of holidays available to workers actually decreased through the turn of the twentieth century. Fitch said, "There are only two holidays in the steel industry today, Christmas and the Fourth of July, and even these are denied to the men of the blast furnace crews." On Labor Day 1907, he passed through towns of closed shops and celebrating families, but the Edgar Thomson plant remained active. "There was a holiday for all except the steel worker," he said.

This left little opportunity for steelworkers to have an outside life. Dust-covered workers trudged out at the end of each twelve-hour shift, stopped at the nearest saloon and silently drank a glass of beer in a line of coworkers. Some drank whiskey to clear their throats, they said, of the dust and ash that caked them. Aside from drinking on the nights after paydays, there was no time to socialize. Few could even attend church, and some developed a bitter attitude toward clergymen who expected them to abstain from liquor and spend their little free time on religious activities. One skilled worker told Fitch:

> *The preachers don't have any influence in securing better conditions for men and they don't try to have. They never visit the mills, and they don't know anything about the conditions that men have to face. They think the men ought to go to church after working twelve hours Sunday night. They could accomplish a lot if they would try to use their influence in the right direction. Let them quit temperance reform until they get better conditions for the men. It is no time to preach to a man when he is hungry.*

All this came as the workers' share of revenue gradually dropped. Many at the mills had long been paid by tonnage; that is, the more they produced, the more they made. Advancing technology meant more steel was being produced than ever before, and bosses cut the workers' rates accordingly. Hard physical labor had given way to speed, and machines placed new strains on workers' bodies and minds. "The result of it [automation] is a system of speeding, unceasing and relentless, seldom equaled in any industry, at any time," Fitch wrote. The steel bosses hoped to place a ceiling on workers' pay in order to produce record tonnage without paying workers at increasing rates. The workers disagreed; the companies were richer than ever before, so why shouldn't they get a growing share for themselves? "There should be an end somewhere to labor standing the brunt of cheapened production," one representative said.

Workers who dreamed of better conditions, a share of the profits, a shorter day and extra pay for hours after eight in a day would have to take matters into their own hands.

"Labor and Capital"

Pittsburgh steelmen had organized for better pay and conditions years before the Clinton Furnace ever towered over the South Side. Beginning in late 1849, the city's puddlers, those who stirred molten iron by hand, had gone on strike against the iron bosses in the industry's first major industrial action. Puddlers' skills were hard to replace, and they knew their value.

When the workers first organized, even the local press stood on their side. The *Pittsburgh Morning Post*'s front page of January 19, 1850, read, "We have never known a set of men more determined to stand out for their rights, and resist oppression, than the honest and industrious operatives in the various mills. They will not yield an inch." An anonymous letter-writer sounded almost like a radical of the next century: "In place of calling it a Puddlers and Boilers strike, it should be called the encroachment of capitalists against labor."

In the end, the capitalists won. The iron bosses cut wages and hired replacements, but Pittsburgh's ironworkers had their first taste of organizing. In the wake of a panic that threatened the industry, a group of puddlers began meeting regularly at a hotel on Diamond Street. It was there, at one of their beery gatherings in 1858, that the city's puddlers established their first union: the Sons of Vulcan. The group began in fits and starts, but the

Civil War improved their fortunes just as it did for Carnegie and the iron bosses. Skyrocketing demand for arms pushed puddlers' wages up, and the Sons of Vulcan launched a national organizing drive to hold onto their gains.

By 1867, two years after the Civil War's end, the Grand Forge National Convention of the Sons of Vulcan met at the corner of Fifth Avenue and Smithfield Street, which was then called the Boilers' Hall. Representatives traveled from as far as Chicago and Kentucky. Workers in the related crafts that made up the early iron industry—heaters, rollers, roughers—gradually organized in their own local lodges, each craft remaining strictly separate. Arguments for amalgamation grew louder, and at a joint Pittsburgh convention in 1876, representatives from across the iron industry voted to merge their crafts into a new union. In a hall draped with the Stars and Stripes and union banners, workers forged their first big union.

The first years of the Amalgamated Association of Iron and Steel Workers, often simply called "the Amalgamated," saw tremendous growth. Relations with the Pittsburgh iron and steel bosses were pleasant enough, and organizers reached many of the region's largest mills and furnaces. Even Carnegie, the symbol of the bosses' wealth and power, expressed support for unions and workers' rights. In an 1886 article, he wrote, "The right of working men to combine and to form trade associations is no less sacred than the right of the manufacturer to enter into associations and conferences with his fellows....My experience has been that trade unions upon the whole are beneficial both to labor and capital." Carnegie's philanthropy seemed well-suited to promote good relations with workers even as he consolidated control over much of the region's iron and steel production.

Below the surface, however, capital and labor were set for a collision. Carnegie had hired the notorious union-buster Henry Clay Frick to oversee business operations. Frick had used immigrant strikebreakers to replace restive workers in the Connellsville coke mines, and in 1891, he oversaw the massacre of coal strikers by the state National Guard. Westmoreland County miners, whose product fed the Carnegie mills, demanded shorter days and better pay, but Frick was confident in the company's victory. "If we succeed in winning on the terms proposed, organizing in the coke region is killed," he told a lieutenant. Frick evicted immigrant workers from company housing and called in the authorities, who shot down at least seven civilians and arrested many of the survivors. The so-called Morewood Massacre would be a dark prelude to the tactics steel bosses would employ in the years to come.

An 1882 magazine portrays a "great labor strike" in Maryland and Pennsylvania with an operational Pittsburgh mill at center. *Library of Congress.*

Frick followed the massacre with a firm hand against workers in Carnegie's Homestead Works. The mill, which employed thousands of skilled and unskilled laborers, held key navy contracts and represented an important piece of the Carnegie empire. But after an 1889 strike left the workers with a favorable contract and broad power over mill operations, Frick set out to regain control. Some sixty pages of contract footnotes gave the workers extra protections and benefits, and as a consequence, Frick believed they failed "to turn out the product they should." By 1891, the Amalgamated had twenty-four thousand members, which accounted for two-thirds of those workers who were eligible to join. Frick knew a victory over them could undo the union throughout the steel district.

In the late nineteenth century, before the wave of New Deal legislation that enshrined organizing and striking rights, many businesses were only partially unionized, as they are in modern "right-to-work" states. This left workers and bosses to argue over the need to recognize a union at all. After all, if only a fraction of the workforce paid dues, the union could be sidelined, and its activists could be easily replaced. Carnegie and Frick saw such an opportunity in Homestead, where the worker-friendly contract was set to expire on June 30, 1892. "Every man will see that the firm cannot run union and non-union," Carnegie wrote Frick as they schemed to break the Homestead Amalgamated. "It must be either one or the other."

A draft notice made clear the bosses' intentions. They would make Homestead a non-union open shop, no matter the cost.

> *These works having been consolidated with the Edgar Thomson and Duquesne, and other mills, there has been forced upon this firm the question whether its works are to be run "union" or "non-union." As the vast majority of our employees are non-union, the firm has decided that the minority must give place to the majority. These works therefore, will be necessarily non-union after the expiration of the present agreement.*

No new agreement was reached, and the company locked the workers out as the contract expired. Word spread through Homestead that Carnegie and Frick planned to offload scabs and armed strikebreakers at the mill, and the news of an impending confrontation spread as far as New York, where it reached the national press. Homestead became a fortress, with armed workers forming militias and Frick hiring gunmen from the feared Pinkerton detective agency. "It is evident that there is to be no 'bluffing' at Homestead," the *New York Times* said. "The fight there is to be to the death

An 1892 magazine cover illustrates the violence at Homestead. The mill lockout and ensuing violent siege was national news. *Library of Congress.*

between the Carnegie Steel Company, Limited, with its $25 million capital, and the workmen."

Gun battles broke out as Carnegie officials sent boatloads of Pinkerton agents across the Monongahela River in a bid to seize and fortify the plant. The armed workers killed three Pinkertons and took more prisoner—a rare and inspiring victory for the labor movement that had so often been on the receiving end of deadly violence.

Their victory was to be short-lived. Frick had advertised across the country for non-union replacement workers, and he now had the armed forces of the government on his side. Twelve days after the lockout began, soldiers of the Pennsylvania militia marched into Homestead and broke through the strikers' lines. Replacement workers reopened the plant, and the Amalgamated was broken.

More than four hundred miles away in Worcester, Massachusetts, a young Russian immigrant read a newspaper article that covered the strike, and his fury rose. Pinkertons had shot innocent civilians outside Pittsburgh. The bosses had turned the mills into fortresses. Frick had declared war on the workers. Alexander Berkman, a twenty-two-year-old man, glanced silently at his longtime girlfriend, Emma Goldman, and his cousin, Modest Aronstam. "We sit in silence, each busy with his own thoughts," he would recall years later. "Only now and then we exchange a word, a searching, significant look." Berkman knew what had to be done.

Raised in Russia under the tsars' absolute dictatorship, Berkman was acquainted from a young age with rebellious ideas that had remained rare in America. There, anarchists, nihilists and narodniks assassinated aristocrats hoping that individual acts of shocking revenge would inspire the people to overthrow the state. Berkman would introduce these ideas of rebellion to the steel barons with gun and knife.

Berkman soon boarded a train to Pittsburgh and imagined the battles in Homestead as he rode. On July 23, well after Carnegie had won the war against the Amalgamated, Berkman walked into Frick's Fifth Avenue office and drew a revolver. "The look of terror on his face strikes me speechless," Berkman later wrote of Frick. "It is the dread of the conscious presence of death. 'He understands,' it flashes through my mind....With a look of horror, he quickly averts his face as I pull the trigger." Berkman shot twice, then set upon him with a dagger before a bystander intervened.

Frick survived; Berkman would spend fourteen years in prison.

Two months after the attack, the *Pittsburgh Press* reported on the courtroom defense of "The Red Berkman." Only a few attended the hearing, but reporters described his "anarchistic tirade," which referenced the killings of labor demonstrators in Chicago six years prior:

> *I belong to those murdered at Chicago...this free spirit cannot be oppressed. It is stronger than your collected police power, and does not bend at your mighty power. This spirit will go from works to works, families to families and will enter into the hearts of all laborers or all lands, and this spark of life of this spirit shall spread over the whole world. This certain fire will grow, and it is childish to oppose this free spirit.*

Reporters mocked his speech, delivered in German, as a "flow of meaningless sentences" and "an inflammatory tirade against capital and on behalf of labor." It may have appeared meaningless in 1892, but in the years to come, words like Berkman's would become far more common in the streets and union halls of Pittsburgh.

The years after Homestead were grim for the Amalgamated. While the militia's bayonets and Frick's Pinkertons had dealt the deadly blow in 1892, the union's own policies helped seal its defeat. Steelmaking was no longer the skilled craft it once was; battalions of unskilled laborers, many of them unable to read or speak English, had largely replaced the tradesmen who once ran puddling mills and blast furnaces. The American Federation of Labor, of which the Amalgamated was a major part, had refused to embrace unskilled workers. Its leaders maintained that craft unionism, the rigid division of workers to ensure control over each sector's specialist labor supply, was the best approach. The effect was clear: at Homestead, during the strike, the union represented only a few hundred of the thousands on the plant's rolls. Its membership was white and largely native-born or western European in an industry that, by 1907 nationwide,

A puddler prepares iron. The labor-intensive method involved rolling molten metal into balls before shaping it into bars. *Library of Congress.*

was one-third Slavic, Hungarian and Italian. In an age of unskilled labor, this made the immigrant workers replaceable.

The union's decline was accelerated as the nation's industries formed into powerful trusts. Tinplate and sheet metal manufacturers were merging, which gave them overwhelming power against organized labor, and the planned formation of U.S. Steel was a potentially fatal blow to the union. Amalgamated membership had already dropped from twenty-four thousand to eight thousand in less than a decade. Leaders knew they had to win a great victory against the newly formed steel trust. They launched a strike against U.S. Steel at its formation in 1901 and failed miserably. Many plants remained open, and Pittsburgh bosses immediately threatened to replace those workers who left. "It was a palpable loss to the workers' cause," the *Pittsburgh Press* reported. "Organized labor received a defeat from which it can recover but slowly." In the end, there were more plants that lost their union representation than those that gained it, and the *Pittsburgh Press* placed the blame squarely on outdated union attitudes. Ten thousand members of the "steel workers' aristocratic union" had dragged eighty thousand workers into their strike, but the union still denied most of them the chance to join, its reporters noted. They weren't fellow union men but victims of the Amalgamated and its refusal to expand.

For many Pittsburgh workers left in the cold, a new group would finally offer the chance to organize. Its purpose was as simple as its name: the One Big Union.

"The Greatest Labor Fight in All History"

A new era began in 1909, at the deadly McKees Rocks Works of Frank Norton Hoffstot's Pressed Steel Car Co. The company works, which produced steel railcars on a fast-moving assembly line, were known for their continual stream of accidents. County Coroner Joseph G. Armstrong testified, "It seemed to me that the deaths averaged about one a day. Many of the deaths resulted from men being struck by heavy moving cranes and the dogs [mechanical devices] suspended from the cranes. Investigation made it look to me as though a lot of young fellows who were operating the cranes did not care much whether a 'hunky' laborer was hit now and then." Investigators and county officials deplored the company's treatment of its deceased workers; in most cases, their families received no more than enough to bury their loved ones, and many got no payment at all. Allegheny

County authorities were left to bury the poor inhabitants of McKees Rocks's "Hunky Town," where immigrants from Croatia, Poland, Lithuania and a dozen other countries lived in hastily built company housing. William E. Trautmann, a New Zealand–born radical organizer who joined the strike, later described the workers' living conditions in a novel:

> *From an isolated elevation yonder, long rows of workers from all directions descend into the valley with dinner pails in their hands; from the depression Preston Hollow, Poles and Lithuanians slowly climb up and pass with their mud-covered shoes over the broad, bare highway, past wall after wall and building after building to the main entrance of the works....Cramped and crowded, mute and dejected, they press together in front of the steel-ribbed, rolling gates. Loud sounds are rarely heard. Their faces stand out, drawn and haggard from anxious suspense. Those who arrive a little too late, as well as the dead and wounded, will be replaced in five minutes after the change of shifts from the ranks of those who wait.*

Peace couldn't last in McKees Rocks. On July 13, 1909—after a payday in which workers had gotten even less than their usual, arbitrarily assigned rates—hundreds, then thousands of workers walked out. Hoffstot hired replacements and mocked the strikers, but the workers quickly took up positions around the town's landmark "Indian Mound" and set in for a long battle. Unlike past labor battles, eastern and southern European immigrants were active in the strike and addressed their comrades from the mound in every language spoken at the plant. News photographs showed knots of men in hats, "waiting to speak to the crowd in different tongues" while police watched on horseback. Armed, helmeted officers marched in from other parts of the state. Many came from as far as Greensburg, and some were veterans of the brutal U.S. campaign against Philippine rebels.

Strikers dismissed the police as "cossacks," no different from the steppe tribesmen who massacred demonstrators in the Russian Empire. Battles broke out across McKees Rocks, with police shooting workers and angry townsfolk bashing officers with tools. "Under a perfect rain of bricks, stones and clubs, the state officers fought their way back and forth from one end of McKees Rocks to the other, surrounded constantly by thousands of infuriated men and women, representing a large portion of the population of McKees Rocks," the *Pittsburgh Press* reported. "Fighting like demons, the strikers pressed the mounted constables so fiercely that in self-defense the officers were forced to use their rifles, several hundred shots being fired before they

Mounted constables wait, guns visible, during a strike—possibly the 1909 McKees Rocks pressed steel strike. *Library of Congress.*

The "bloody corner" in McKees Rocks was a scene of fighting during the 1909 pressed steel strike. *Library of Congress.*

succeeded in beating off their assailants." Attempts to land strikebreakers by boat failed, just as they had failed in Homestead seventeen years earlier.

But unlike the Homestead strikers, the McKees Rocks strikers hailed from all nationalities and didn't rely on the Amalgamated to lead them. While American-born and English-speaking workers organized and negotiated separately, many plant workers joined a new group—the Industrial Workers of the World (IWW). Founded just four years prior, the IWW, commonly called the Wobblies, fought for industrial unionism with armies of unskilled workers joining together to conquer entire industries. Their ideology ranged from the militant anarchism of Berkman, Frick's would-be assassin, to the scientific socialism of Karl Marx. Wobblies and their syndicalist allies believed all workers should join in "one big union" that would become a grand army more powerful than all the world's capitalists. Soon to be famous for its "Little Red Songbook" and its organization of itinerant workers, the IWW had already achieved successes in the western states at the time of the McKees Rocks strike. IWW members stood in firm opposition to what they considered the milquetoast craft unionism of the American Federation of Labor (AFL). The AFL would never challenge capitalism at its core, while the IWW called openly for "the abolition of the wage system."

Wobbly organizers swept into western Pennsylvania and set up shop amongst the pressed steel workers. Their members included Trautmann, the New Zealander, and other famous leaders like William "Big Bill" Haywood, a titan of American organizing. Their New Castle local established a weekly newspaper called *Solidarity*. Its slogan said, "The workshop is the most important thing in society. Whoever controls the shop controls society. Get wise." Under IWW leadership, the McKees Rocks workers pursued their cause for weeks, even as workers, police officers and sheriff's deputies died in battle.

Their cause soon drew attention from across the country. Eugene Debs, the fiery leader of the Socialist Party, traveled to McKees Rocks in late August to address a throng of workers from the Indian Mound:

> *There are fifteen nationalities represented here this morning, but you are of one class. You are workmen, united in a single cause. You are wage slaves in the eyes of the corporation. Though I cannot understand your language I can read your hearts and can make myself understood to you… this desperate fight must be continued. The eyes of the civilized world and the eyes of all the laborers of the world are upon you. It is the greatest labor fight in all history.*

Eugene Debs, five-time presidential candidate and founding member of the Socialist Party of America and the Industrial Workers of the World, addresses a rally crowd. *Library of Congress.*

Debs's words would have sounded unfamiliar, even laughable, in Pittsburgh strikes just a generation earlier, but in 1909, workers of all nationalities were prepared to organize. Even the Amalgamated would soon take note. With help from allied unions across Pittsburgh, the McKees Rocks workers won several concessions, which included an end to arbitrary pay systems, raises and a return to work for union men, among other things. "It had been thought that the Slavs were too sluggish to resist their employers, and unable to organize along industry lines," Fitch, the New York labor investigator, wrote. "It was proved in this conflict that neither theory was correct; and, stranger still, it was demonstrated that American-born and immigrant workmen can and will work side by side for common ends." In 1910, the Amalgamated formally amended its constitution to end its craft focus and adopt an industry-wide organization scheme. Initiation fees were halved, and leaders reached out—in fits and starts—to foreign-born workers. "There is but one way to relieve [the] situation for the men in the iron and steel industries. That is to organize them into a powerful organization, embracing all the branches of the steel and iron industry, beginning with the blast furnaces," said one Amalgamated leader.

The clannish jealousy of the Sons of Vulcan and the Homestead strikers was giving way to the solidarity of Debs, Trautmann and Haywood. Across Pittsburgh and its neighboring towns, their radical ideas were fast taking root in labor schools, socialist summer camps and secret, radical meetings.

"Workers of the World, Unite!"

Samuel Mervis (sometimes spelled Mirvis) shouted as the police dragged him from a platform at the corner of Kelly Street and Homewood Avenue.

"This is Russianized America!" yelled the bespectacled twenty-nine-year-old cigar maker as officers rounded up dozens of his fellow socialists and hauled them to jail. It was a bold statement, comparing the police to the cossacks and soldiers who massacred Russia's poor in the name of the tsar. The socialists were charged with speaking publicly without a permit, and when a magistrate heard their case, the courtroom was filled with socialist debate. In a Frankstown Avenue holding cell that night, prisoners asked newcomers, "Are you a comrade?" and joined in revolutionary songs.

A talented orator, Mervis was one of several socialists assigned by local party officers to address street corners across the city. It was election season in the summer of 1912, and reporters described crowds of thousands at socialist speaking engagements. In Homewood, a popular site for the public addresses, police soon warned the local officials of the Socialist Party of America that they would have to cancel their speech if they could not get permits.

"A flood of handbills informed the district that the meeting would be held anyhow," the *Pittsburgh Press* reported. When a crowd of hundreds arrived on August 10 to hear Mervis, police surged in and arrested the most raucous among them. The offenders were soon released. Just a few days later, Mervis stood atop a soapbox at the same Homewood intersection. Police again showed up, demanded a permit and hauled Mervis away. The reason for Mervis's arrest, officials said, was clear: the socialists failed to get the proper paperwork, and they refused to accept alternate sites recommended by police.

The socialists had their own theory for the repression. A local legislative race was heating up, and their candidates threatened the status quo. "We will take the clubs from the police," a seventeen-year-old prisoner reportedly said. "Then we will use them on the heads of the capitalistic class!" There was no denying it; in Allegheny County and across the

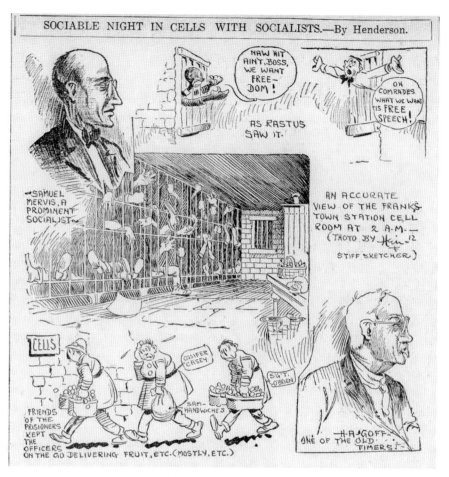

A 1912 cartoon in the *Pittsburgh Daily Post*—"Sociable Night in Cells with Socialists"—makes light of the mass arrest of socialist demonstrators in the East End. Pittsburgh Daily Post *via Newspapers.com.*

country, anti-capitalism was firmly in the mainstream, and socialist rallies readily drew thousands.

In elections that fall, radical candidates fared better than they had at any time in American history. Socialists drew more than nine hundred thousand votes nationwide in 1912, and Eugene Debs, who had addressed striking workers in McKees Rocks just three years earlier, got 6 percent of the vote. In Allegheny County, Debs drew nearly twenty thousand votes—more than 15 percent of the total. The story was the same across western Pennsylvania and eastern Ohio, where slates of socialist candidates ran for every position, from coroner to judge to congressman. These candidates, who were generally election-minded and sometimes dismissed as "slowcialists" by their more revolutionary comrades, sought welfare and business reforms in the spirit of the progressivism that was sweeping the country. They had won early successes in a handful of cities; in Milwaukee, the Austrian-immigrant congressman Victor Berger spearheaded "sewer socialism," which was a reform ideology in which public health projects and infrastructure improvements would pave the way to the end of capitalism. Candidates in Berger's mold even enjoyed success in small cities like Altoona, where a socialist councilman pushed for trash pickup and financial reforms.

The Socialist Party saw some of its greatest success in New Castle, where candidates swept onto the council and took the mayor's seat in 1912. Mayor Walter Tyler used his bully pulpit in the press to call for class equality. In a letter to the *New Castle News*, he argued:

> *It has been said that the same law which applies to a workingman cannot be used against a public service corporation. That may have been true in the past, but I'll assure citizens that if complaints are lodged at the proper time, that the police powers of this city will be used to see that the rights of the people are not trampled underfoot.*

That year, nearly 17 percent of voters backed socialism at the top of the ticket in Lawrence County, where the IWW newspaper, *Solidarity*, was soon joined by a Socialist Party paper, the *Free Press*.

It comes as little surprise that the ideology quickly made inroads among steelworkers, even those who did not join the unions. As Ed Jones, a skilled worker in a Pittsburgh mill, told Fitch:

> *It is of no use for them to try to regulate wages anyway, for labor is a commodity and its price is regulated by supply and demand. The only way out for the laboring men is to get together in a labor party....We must go back to the condition when workmen owned their own tools. We must own the instruments of production. Labor is now the helpless victim of capital, and capital must be overthrown. The workman is given enough to buy food and clothes for himself, and no more if the capitalist can help himself. They keep the workmen employed twelve hours a day at some work, while if every man in the country would work two hours a day, all the labor that would be necessary to support the population of the country could be performed. Now all of this excess, this ten hours over the necessary amount, goes to the employer in profits, and many*

people throughout the country are living in idleness because other people are working overtime for them.

The fact that a steelworker, one who was orphaned in New York and sent to Pittsburgh for a life in the mills, could detail the theories of Karl Marx demonstrates the mainstream popularity of socialism before World War I. The party grew quickly, counting more than twelve thousand dues-paying members in Pennsylvania by 1912. But it wasn't only in the dues ledgers and at the ballot box where the Socialist Party of America succeeded. In Pittsburgh, the movement built a cultural base that left its mark on the city's politics, its immigrant societies and even on its architecture.

By 1912, a weekly "Socialist Bulletin" appeared in the *Pittsburgh Press*, and it dutifully reported the minutiae of meetings and social functions over several columns. Appearing in the bulletin were advertisements for box socials, picnics and swimming sessions, all under the formal auspices of the party. "At 4 p.m. a baseball game will take place between the Socialist teams from the Northside and the Southside," a 1913 issue noted. "The Southsiders are confident of a victory, as they claim all their players are in good shape,

A poster advertises Socialist Party candidate Eugene Debs in 1904. Debs surged in 1912, garnering an unprecedented share of the vote. *Library of Congress.*

and the Northside boys are making the same claim, so a hot contest is assured." The bulletin regularly advertised trolley trips to farms and parks outside the city, where comrades could relax and drink together on holidays. An item on a 1916 encampment at Conneaut Lake boasted that "a continuous round of amusements, educational features [and] athletic events keep the campers continually on the go." The Young People's Socialist League, affectionately called the "Yipsels," organized camping trips and dances for the younger comrades. "You are all cordially invited to come and bring your friends to meet these live young wires of the Socialist movement," a 1918 item said. "The Yipsel dances are always top-notch in character, the music furnished for these affairs always being of the very best." A book called *Songs for Young Socialists* included tunes like "Father Is a Socialist," "When Yipsel Dreams Come True" and "Kid Comrades."

The socialists, along with both friendly and competing labor and immigrant groups, met at a string of offices across Pittsburgh. There was New Era Hall at 233 Fifth Avenue, where party officials met, union organizers addressed workers and Yipsels taught Socialist Sunday School.

A 1916 piece in the *Pittsburgh Daily Post* shows the construction of the Jewish Labor Lyceum, which would house a collection of radical and union groups for years. Pittsburgh Daily Post *via Newspapers.com.*

The Jewish Labor Lyceum, built in 1916 at the corner of Reed and Miller Streets in the Hill District, before its demolition circa 2018. *Courtesy of Angelique Bamberg.*

Neighborhood and borough socialist groups met at fraternal halls and rented their own offices. Several city wards and districts were home to their own Socialist Party chapters, where officers kept meticulous monthly records of dues payments. In the Hill District, where Yiddish-speaking Jewish immigrants formed the backbone of the socialist movement and some of the local unions, backers laid the cornerstone of the Jewish Labor Lyceum in 1916. The Lyceum, near the corner of Miller and Reed Streets, hosted an ever-changing array of leftist newspapers, union offices and Jewish groups until internal left-wing battles later reduced its significance. The building was recognizable by its cornerstone, which bore Marx's call to arms: "Workers of the World, Unite." The Hill's Jewish activists carried on their own battles as the steel towns heated up; garment workers met at the Lyceum, stogie rollers joined the IWW to fight for raises and kosher bakers organized to end night work.

The more radical activists, including those who didn't speak English, opened their own spaces in Pittsburgh. The IWW maintained a "radical library" in the McGeagh Building, an office tower at 607 Bigelow Boulevard, where it soon drew the attention of the authorities. In 1918, immigrants raised more than $18,000 to buy a property they called International Socialist Lyceum at the corner of James and Foreland Streets on the North Side. This purchase was so large that it even alarmed the federal investigators tasked with tracking the city's radicals.

By 1914, even the most extreme elements of the labor movement had mass appeal, or at least mass interest. A half-page article in the *Pittsburgh Press* "Illustrated Sunday Magazine" section—set alongside a fluffy spring fashion piece—detailed the lives and views of the IWW's "Red Angels," who occupied churches and battled the police. A female member of the One Big Union expounded in the pages of a mainstream city paper:

> *The working class and the capitalist class have nothing in common. The employers have no rights (as employers) which the workers are bound to respect. We yield only because they have the guns and we do not wish to die. We must live to do our part in fulfilling the historic mission of the working class—the overthrow of the capitalist class.*

Downtown Pittsburgh circa 1913. In the background is the McGeagh Building, which housed the IWW "radical library" that was raided by investigators during a nationwide sweep. *Pittsburgh city photographer via Historic Pittsburgh.*

Beneath the appearance of coming victory, deep fissures were already forming in the Socialist Party. In Pittsburgh and across the country, militant activists were splitting from the "slowcialists," who believed in gradual political reform. This was clear in Pittsburgh's *Socialist Bulletin*, where early debates quickly turned to expulsions and denunciations. Samuel Mervis, who was twice arrested in 1912 for his Homewood street speeches, was represented in court by a radical Pittsburgh attorney, Jacob Margolis. Just a few months later, Margolis and Mervis faced off in a public debate on "sabotage and direct action," tactics favored by groups like the IWW but dismissed by many of the more election-minded members of the Socialist Party. While the socialists called for reforms from above, instituted by elected officials, the IWW and its supporters rejected piecemeal bargaining and called for workers to block up the system of production. By mid-1913, the *Socialist Bulletin* included warnings against a "short cut to socialism"—an obvious knock on the radicals who called for a "grand physical revolution, folding of arms, general strike or anarchy."

That year, the Allegheny County Socialist Party expelled some four hundred of its members, including Fred Merrick, the editor of the local socialist newspaper, for supporting "sabotage." As the clouds of war gathered in Europe and Pittsburgh awaited its own revolutionary wave, a growing radical movement was forming its own, even more militant, branches. These militants, with their belief in industrial unionism, mass action and organization across ethnic and language barriers, were already working to organize steelworkers. Their ideas were given a voice by a IWW "Red Angel" who appeared in the *Pittsburgh Press*.

> *The rise of great machinery, which involves the concentration of capital, has completely revolutionized the economic world. But capitalism, which must fall with its institutions, keeps up the farce of carrying on this new industrial government through the ghosts of old constitutions and laws. Thus, all is chaos. Production is run mad. The workers are in the breadlines because they have not yet learned that they are the world.*
>
> *But they will learn. This is inevitable. For the present institution there is no remedy but the overthrow of capitalism.*

2

THE ORGANIZING WAR

The roar of guns in Europe changed everything in the principality of steel. When Serbia and Austria-Hungary went to war in summer 1914, they drew in a web of alliances and sparked brutal fighting across French farmland, Polish forests and far-flung colonies. For the neutral United States, the war was an economic boon. By 1916, foreign trade was nearly double the annual averages from 1911 to 1914, and exports to Europe surged past previous records. The warring powers needed raw materials and munitions, and American companies were happy to oblige them. No industry was more important to the war effort than steel. Revenue skyrocketed; in 1914, U.S. Steel tallied a financial reserve of $135 million, but by 1917, it had grown to $431 million. Furnaces, mills and finishing plants ran at full blast, churning out armored plating for ships and metal components for shells and weapons.

However, the war also halted the flow of a key resource for Pittsburgh's steel titans. Workers from eastern Europe—the Russian and Austro-Hungarian empires, as well as Serbia, Greece, Italy and Romania—were stranded by blockades or conscripted in their own homelands. The Croats, Hungarians, Slovaks and Poles, who might have otherwise been working in Pittsburgh mills, were now dying by the thousands in Galicia and East Prussia.

The demand for workers, coupled with the dwindling labor supply, left the bosses with few options. Pittsburgh workers wanted a share of the new profits, and even in their unorganized state, some were willing to fight. When bosses dismissed a union supporter at a Westinghouse Electric Corp. factory in April 1916, thousands of workers walked off the job and launched a weeks-long battle that left several dead and drew militia regiments from across the state. On May Day, crowds of workers staged a demonstration outside the Edgar Thomson Works in Braddock; "intoxicated foreigners" would later try to storm the gates and draw the steelworkers to their cause, the *Pittsburgh Press* claimed. A *Gazette Times* article described the chaos at the Braddock mill: "Police interference was brushed aside. When the Braddock police attempted to arrest a man, they were turned on and under a rain of stones were forced to release their prisoner….The rioting lasted for nearly three hours and did not cease until strike leaders persuaded the strikers to disperse." Angry Westinghouse workers called on their comrades in steel to join them, and a few walked off or left under threat, newspapers claimed. Government power eventually quelled the Westinghouse riots. The steelworkers didn't rise up en masse as some had hoped, but when the United States declared war on Germany and its allies a year later, pressures on the steel industry would increase.

The U.S. declaration of war turned the screws on the steel barons, who now faced unprecedented labor shortages alongside massive government orders. Tens of thousands of workers volunteered and were called up for service in Europe, which left those who remained in a better bargaining position. One manager at Youngstown Sheet and Tube, a smaller company outside of U.S. Steel, said he could expect only twelve thousand of his

Recruits train in Oakmont during World War I. A wave of patriotism overtook the country as thousands of soldiers prepared to fight in France. *Oakmont Carnegie Library via Historic Pittsburgh.*

fourteen thousand employees to show up on any given day. Many workers knew their importance to the company, and a day off was sometimes more valuable to them than another long shift. "The men want a day off to have a good time for recreation, or for one reason or another," said the manager.

While workers held more power than they had before the war, this pressure ran in both directions. The steel companies were desperate for men—any men—to keep the machines running day and night. If anything, twelve-hour days and seven-day weeks became more common, and they weren't optional. By 1919, those working in blast furnaces in the Pittsburgh steel district averaged eighty-two hours per week and those in open-hearth furnaces averaged seventy-six. A worker at the Homestead plant detailed his daily routine for investigators from a Protestant church organization:

> *5:30 [p.m.] to 12 (midnight)—Six and one-half hours of shoveling, throwing and carrying bricks and cinder out of bottom of old furnace. Very hot.*
> *12:30—Back to the shovel and cinder, within few feet of pneumatic shovel drilling slag, for three and one-half hours.*
> *4 o'clock—Sleeping is pretty general, including boss.*
> *5 o'clock—Everybody quits, sleeps, sings, swears, sighs for 6 o'clock.*
> *6 o'clock—Start home.*
> *6:45 o'clock—Bathed, breakfast.*
> *7:45 o'clock—Asleep.*
> *4 P.M.—Wake up, put on dirty clothes, go to boarding house, eat supper, get pack of lunch.*
> *5:30 P.M.—Report for work.*

These shifts left little time for family life; one Johnstown worker said his infant died but that "he had never known the child because he was at work whenever she was awake." Steel bosses claimed they ran long, round-the-clock shifts by necessity, but union supporters and progressive allies said they could easily run eight-hour shifts or close the mills during certain hours. The only clear argument for the long shifts, limited days off and twenty-four- to thirty-six-hour turns was that they produced more steel and thus made more money.

World War I left its mark on the workforce. The "hunkies," many of whom had once planned to return home with money in their pockets, now found themselves stuck indefinitely in the United States. The demand for their jobs, even the unskilled ones, and the sense that they were producing arms for a patriotic cause left many feeling like true Americans, even if Pittsburgh newspapers carelessly lumped Slavic labor activists together with the enemy by calling them "Austrians."

The mill bosses drew from previously untapped sources for their labor, and by the war's end, hundreds of thousands of black workers from the South had moved to northern and midwestern cities to churn out steel. African Americans made up nearly 11 percent of Pennsylvania's steel workforce, and they occupied an even larger percentage in other states. Once dismissed as scabs and strikebreakers, African American workers still contended with discrimination and were frequently rejected from union activities. Bosses and fellow workers derided their high turnover rates. "You have to employ ten negroes in the course of a year in order to keep one on the job," one investigator said, citing comments he had collected. Eugene Kinckle Jones, a renowned black social worker and activist, offered an explanation for this:

> *The negro in such a position usually has no hope on the job, as a group. They do not aspire to anything higher than the unskilled work, because they realize the door of opportunity to them is closed….Not only are they discriminated against generally by the men who do not want them to work in certain positions where the wages are good and conditions are better than the average, but even the foremen, and I might say the superintendents themselves, have discriminated against them.*

The president of Inland Steel would offer a blunt confirmation of this discrimination after the war: "The negroes should remain in the South." Even in the face of long hours and stagnant compensation against sky-high profits, the steelworkers remained divided.

The wartime boom improved some immigrant workers' conditions, but many still lived in overcrowded homes without indoor plumbing. Feeding and clothing children ate up much of workers' meager incomes; one worker's wife told investigators she spent ten dollars each month on children's shoes, which left herself barefoot. Some workers were encouraged to pay inflated prices at company stores. Others reported to investigators that they had to frequent their landlords' businesses for fear of eviction. Steel companies built modern housing for workers in newer cities, but in the Pittsburgh river valleys, most workers remained in battered old houses in low-lying immigrant neighborhoods. The workers' proud wives insisted on keeping clean white curtains in their windows,

A wartime poster by artist Gerrit Beneker shows a patriotic worker promising his support in the fight against Germany. *Library of Congress.*

the journalist Mary Heaton Vorse observed, as a tiny symbol of control even in smog-choked steel towns like Braddock.

> *The courts are bricked and littered with piles of cans, piles of rubbish, bins of garbage, hillocks of refuse—refuse and litter, litter and refuse. Playing in the refuse and ashes and litter—children. The decencies of life ebb away as one nears the mills…no green thing grew anywhere… generation after generation of children, born where no green thing grows. Hundreds and thousands of children playing in the refuse of forsaken brick courtyards or along the streets. Generations of children reared under the somber magnificence of the clouds of smoke which blanket the sky and obscure the sun.*

STEEL BOSSES AND COMPANY UNIONS

The war may have raised wages, but prices continued to rise, and life remained hard for the twelve-hour-a-day men and their families.

This posed a problem for President Woodrow Wilson. The nation was mobilized for war, and high prices coupled with low wages meant labor unrest, which would mean equipment shortages for the boys in France. With former president William Howard Taft at the helm, Wilson established the National War Labor Board in spring 1918 to ensure labor peace. The board included representatives in equal numbers from major wartime industries and from organized labor, and its proclamations on workers' rights and conditions quickly alarmed the steel bosses who had ruled for years without any serious challenge to their power.

Chief among these alarmed steel bosses was Judge Elbert Gary, head of U.S. Steel and namesake of the company town of Gary, Indiana. A longtime lawyer and justice known as a deeply serious man and a teetotaler, Gary had controlled America's steel trust during an era in which union power was almost nonexistent. He and his fellow executives occasionally worked alongside labor leaders, but they generally ran non-union, open shops and relied on paternalism and welfare programs to keep workers satisfied. Now came an array of federal agencies and investigators, including the rising liberal lawyer Felix Frankfurter, to encourage unionism and improve conditions in the name of victory. Steel executives were horrified—who were these government lawyers to tell them they had to bargain with a union? When Frankfurter proposed a so-called basic eight-hour day, one in which

Judge Elbert Gary, chairman of U.S. Steel during the strike. Gary favored company welfare and stood for the open shop. *Library of Congress.*

steelworkers would get overtime after eight hours but could still work twelve if needed, Gary dismissed the plan as "a sham" and "a method of obtaining a wage increase under false pretenses." Steel men suspected a government plot to install unions in their mills. Foreign observers reacted with astonishment to the steel bosses' resistance to even simple reforms. Vorse said:

> *In Washington I met one of the Dutch employers. "What a surprising country," he said, and he shook with laughter. "I am back in the stone age. Here I find you have not settled the question of collective bargaining. What a country!" He chuckled to himself. He could not understand it....But Mr. Gary of the United States Steel Corporation felt himself a champion of the right of individual bargaining, stemming the incoming flood of organized labor. He felt himself a crusader. He received letters of congratulation from chambers of commerce, from employers' and manufacturers' associations, from the heads of big business concerns.*

Gary and his colleagues had their own methods of keeping union sentiment below the surface. Few inspired more hatred among dedicated organizers than company unions, the employer-run organizations that purported to represent steelworkers' interests while occupying activists' precious time and attention. Deprived of money for strikes and kept under close company watch, these bodies could never challenge the steel bosses seriously. "They consist merely of committees, made up for the most part of hand-picked bosses and 'company suckers,'" a top steel organizer wrote. "There is no real organization of the workers....Company unions are invariably contemptible." For years they had represented the only official outlet for grievances or complaints since the independent unions were weak, undermanned and represented only a tiny fraction of the industry.

But as the war reached its final, bloody months, organizers across the country saw a new chance; once and for all, they would gather America's hundreds of thousands of steelworkers in a mighty union drive and break the power of the industry that many believed was unbreakable. Their efforts would end in the grandest labor battle America had yet seen.

Chicago, 1918

William Z. Foster spent little time celebrating after the greatest victory of his career. The tall, slim American Federation of Labor organizer was known to friends as a serious man who was unselfish and dedicated but who was not suited to parties. He had just won a raft of reforms for the meatpacking workers in Chicago, where the nation's cattle were herded into sprawling industrial districts for slaughter. Foster had led a great organizing drive in the preceding months and threatened a strike that would cripple the nation's meat industries. The federal government was loath to see a strike in such a key area, and on March 30, 1918, a judge handed down a ruling that granted many of the workers' concessions. Among their demands were raises, overtime and the hard-fought-for eight-hour day.

William Z. Foster, secretary-treasurer of the National Committee for Organizing Iron and Steel Workers. Foster worked both in the mainstream AFL and in more radical groups. *Library of Congress.*

Foster quickly picked his next target: steel, the nation's most powerful, and arguably its most union-resistant, industry. As a socialist and syndicalist in the earlier part of the twentieth century, Foster had fought with the IWW before forming his own radical union movement. His 1913 pamphlet, *Syndicalism*, was printed on a bright red cover and detailed his movement's plan to "overthrow capitalism and reorganize society." Foster's organizing talent and hatred of capitalism had been sharpened in his youth while he held a series of odd jobs as a lumberer, sailor and streetcar operator, among others. He eventually took up a job with the AFL, where the leaders were less sympathetic to his radical leanings, so he took to organizing workers along more traditional lines.

Foster saw great promise in steel.

> *The demand for soldiers and munitions had made labor scarce; the Federal administration was friendly; the right to organize was freely conceded by the government and even insisted upon; the steel industry was the master-clock of the whole war program and had to be kept in operation at all costs; the workers were taking new heart and making demands.*

A week after the Chicago meatpacking victory, Foster sent a resolution to AFL leaders demanding a nationwide steel drive:

> *WHEREAS, the organization of the vast armies of wage-earners employed in the steel industries is vitally necessary to the further spread of industrial democracy in America, and*
> *WHEREAS, Organized Labor can accomplish this great task only by putting forth a tremendous effort; therefore be it*
> *RESOLVED, that the executive officers of the A.F. of L. stand instructed to call a conference during this convention of delegates of all international unions whose interests are involved in the steel industries, and of all the State Federations of City Central bodies in the steel districts, for the purpose of uniting all these organizations into one mighty drive to organize the steel plants of America.*

The AFL unanimously adopted Foster's plan in June 1918, but the hard part had just begun. While the Amalgamated had always represented the bulk of those who were considered steelworkers—the furnace operators and finishing men—there were thousands more who fell under the jurisdiction of other unions. No great steel drive would succeed without the cooperation of every union member connected to the industry, from the shippers who hauled ore over the Great Lakes to the men who operated steam shovels and trains at the mills. However, this was the AFL, not the "One Big Union," and each craft jealously protected its interests. In August, the AFL approved new, uniform initiation fees for dozens of unions to encourage the drive. It also asked each participating group to contribute funds and organizers to the movement. Those who participated were then considered members of the newly created National Committee for Organizing Iron and Steel Workers, a body that, by itself, represented half of the union workers in the United States. This committee included members from the International Brotherhood of Electrical Workers, the Quarry Workers' International Union, the Bricklayers', Masons' and Plasterers' International Union and at least twenty more, with even more set to join later. "This group of unions, lined up to do battle with the Steel Trust, represents the largest body of workers ever engaged in a joint union movement in any country," Foster wrote. "The members number approximately two million."

A metal badge features the emblem of the Amalgamated Association of Iron, Steel and Tin Workers. The clasped-hands symbol remains popular among unions and socialist groups today. *Author's collection.*

Foster and his AFL colleagues had high hopes for the national committee, but they soon realized they would have to start small. The participating unions contributed only a paltry one hundred dollars each and offered a "corporal's guard" of professional organizers. Already based largely in Chicago, Foster and his fellow organizers would start their work there before expanding their efforts to other parts of the country. They held "monster meetings" in Chicago, Joliet, Illinois and Gary, Indiana, signing up hundreds of new union men at a time, but U.S. Steel moved quickly to undercut both organizing efforts and government pressure.

In late September, Gary and his fellow U.S. Steel officials announced an unprecedented move: they would unilaterally accept the basic eight-hour day, and they would pay steelworkers time-and-a-half for each hour worked beyond that limit. Workers still had no choice in how long they spent in the mills, but they would get the equivalent of two extra hours of pay each shift. "More than 100,000 steel workers in the immediate Pittsburgh district will benefit by the new plan; 50,000 of this number are on the payroll of the Carnegie Steel Company alone," the *Pittsburgh Post* reported. "Approximately 250,000 workers will benefit if all the independent steel companies follow the lead of the corporation." The Carnegie division of U.S. Steel spent $400,000 each day in payroll, the newspaper said, and the basic eight-hour day would increase that by 14 percent. The workers celebrated, but Foster recognized the move as a ploy to stop unionism before it spread. "Had the [organizing] work been going on everywhere when Mr. Gary attempted this move, the workers would have understood his motives and joined the unions en masse—the unions would have won hands down," Foster said. "But with operations confined to one district, he was able to steal the credit from the unions....No doubt he thought he had dealt it a mortal blow."

Nevertheless, even industry-friendly newspapers recognized that the basic eight-hour day was just one of many demands. Steelworkers wouldn't be placated with a few extra hours of pay each week; some complained that the long hours away from family weren't worth the extra money. Recognizing that progress often begets more progress, the AFL organizers set their plan to attack the Pittsburgh steel district into motion.

On October 1, Foster moved the committee's office from Chicago to the Magee building in downtown Pittsburgh. He said the city was the "industrial labyrinth, the den of the steel trust," where he estimated that at least 70 percent of the nation's steel industry was based. The organizers' plan was to encircle Pittsburgh from the outside in outlying cities and towns before gradually moving into the heart of the district. A frontal assault on the heart of U.S. Steel would have been suicide, as left-wing writer Floyd Dell noted: "Pittsburgh does not represent ordinary capitalism, the capitalism that bickers and dickers with organized labor. Pittsburgh is capitalism militant—capitalism armed to the teeth and carrying a chip on its shoulder."

The outer principalities of steel were scattered across the country, in Milwaukee, Buffalo and even Pueblo, Colorado. Surrounding Pittsburgh was a ring of industrial towns: Ellwood City, Johnstown, Farrell, New Castle and Youngstown, Ohio. On the Monongahela River, where the city was fed coal and coke by barge and train, were the main bastions of steel production: McKeesport, Clairton, Rankin, Duquesne, Braddock, Homestead and the city of Pittsburgh itself. More plants and finishing mills lined the Allegheny and Ohio Rivers above and below the city.

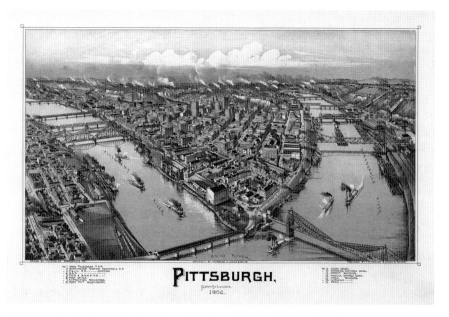

PITTSBURGH.
PENNSYLVANIA.
1902.

A 1902 rendering shows Pittsburgh in its industrial era, with towering office buildings downtown and mills belching smoke far to the east. *Library of Congress.*

The union organizers devised an effective method to handle the surge of union interest they found as they fanned out across Pennsylvania and Ohio. At each "monster mass meeting" in an outlying city, they would meet with local union supporters, form Iron and Steel Workers' Councils, circulate a newsletter in several languages and sign up new members for three dollars apiece. New members would later be directed to their own unions depending on trade, but by then, they would have already experienced the power of mass organizing across craft lines. Foster wrote:

> *The tremendous number of men involved; their unfamiliarity with the English language and total lack of union experience; the wide scope of the operations; the complications created by a score of international unions... the need for quick action in the face of incessant attacks from the Steel Trust—all together produced technical difficulties without precedent.*

As they approached Pittsburgh, the organizers came upon increasingly tough resistance from the bosses and local officials. "Each town produced its own particular crop of problems," Foster said.

JOHNSTOWN

Life in Johnstown revolved around the Cambria Steel Co. The company was once a major competitor to Carnegie, but by 1918, it was only a subsidiary of the Philadelphia-based Midvale Steel and Ordnance Co. Johnstown is located deep in a valley that was formed by the meeting of two rivers, and it had just recovered from its 1889 flood as a gritty, multiethnic industrial town. Workers who lost their jobs would have little hope of staying in the city, and the bosses didn't tolerate even a hint of unionism.

In September 1918, as the organizing drive was just getting underway and as U.S. Steel announced the basic eight-hour day, Cambria Steel officials announced a "representation plan" for its workers in place of a union. Workers would elect representatives to a series of committees, which would then meet with management to discuss grievances. "One evening, soon after the men had gone to work, they were called together to listen to a speech by the superintendent," a labor investigator reported. "The superintendent told them to elect representatives for a meeting in Philadelphia. The men did not understand the purpose of the plan and did not have any chance to formulate their demands but elected hastily chosen representatives on the spot."

Union supporters knew it was a scheme to stop them, but rather than reject the committee outright, they encouraged their fellow workers to support activists and demand the eight-hour day. "No sooner was the result known, however, than the Company discharged the representatives in question," investigators wrote. After this, the workers and bosses were in open conflict, as Foster described:

> *Never was a policy of industrial frightfulness more diabolically conceived or more rigorously executed than that of the Cambria Steel Company. The men sacrificed were the Company's oldest and best employees. Men who had worked faithfully for ten, twenty or thirty years were discharged at a moment's notice. The plan was to pick out men economically most helpless; men who were old and crippled, or who had large families dependent upon them, or homes half paid for, and make examples of them to frighten the rest.*

These attacks only emboldened Cambria's workers, who signed up in ever-greater numbers for the union. In August 1919, after nearly a year of back-and-forth fighting, the company gathered its loyal representatives in

Women picketers distribute literature outside mill property circa 1919. Location unknown. *Library of Congress.*

Atlantic City, "wined and dined them and flattered them" and got them to sign a formal claim that the company's problems could be solved by more production instead of by better pay and conditions. It was the last straw. "This resolution so enraged the Cambria employees after their long attempt to obtain the eight-hour day that most of the highly skilled and highly paid men who had hitherto held aloof from the union, joined them," an investigator wrote. "It is stated that two thousand men signed application blanks immediately after this resolution was published."

DONORA

In the Monongahela Valley, the AFL established a "Flying Squadron" to battle the authorities during its organizing drive. Throughout the valley, the steel companies held the power, and in many cases, burgesses, mayors and council members were directly affiliated with the industry. Organizers lamented the "free-speech deadlock" that kept them from meeting publicly in small towns and cities. In Donora, miles above Pittsburgh on the Monongahela River, AFL official William Feeney found it difficult to organize the workers with the American Steel and Wire Co; the bosses would schedule conflicting events, and the town government had passed ordinances that all but banned public meetings for the union. Feeney rented buildings for his gatherings, Foster recalled, but it was an uphill battle. "In Pennsylvania the Constitution is considered a sort of humorous essay; hence the lickspittle Donora council, right in the face of the steel campaign, passed an ordinance forbidding public meetings without the sanction of the Burgess, which, of course, the unions could not get."

The unions kept up their fight, and before long, their message had taken hold in the minds of the immigrant workers. The local Lithuanian fraternal society ousted its anti-union leaders and replaced them with allies, Foster reported, and skeptical American-born workers told reporters that they perceived far stronger organization among the immigrants. A boycott and internal government disputes opened the path for the organizers. "And thus," Foster said, "free speech and free assembly were established in the benighted town of Donora."

CLAIRTON

In the collection of Monongahela towns that would one day merge to form the city of Clairton, the mill police were closely tied to the government. Officials issued proclamations banning unauthorized meetings and parades, and citizens were ordered to "aid and assist to the fullest extent" in the enforcement of anti-union ordinances. "Burgess Williams of North Clairton, chief of the Carnegie mill police at that point, swore dire vengeance against the free speech fighters should they come to his town," Foster said. One Sunday afternoon, police broke up a public meeting "with a great flourish of clubs." Organizers told Vorse, the journalist, of the fights that happened there:

> We couldn't hold a meeting in Clairton; we couldn't get a permit. We hired an empty lot from a striker and held a meeting there. The Cossacks broke it up. They tore down an American flag. They trampled it under their horses' hoofs. That started trouble with the ex-service boys. Seven [were] arrested and fined. But…even if he was drunk what made him tear down the flag?

MCKEESPORT

McKeesport's mayor, George H. Lysle, was among the organizers' staunchest opponents. As soon as the AFL appeared in town, he issued orders that barred public meetings and threatened mass arrests. In February 1919, Pennsylvania governor William Cameron Sproul pleaded with Lysle to loosen his grip after labor leaders issued a litany of complaints. AFL head Samuel Gompers told the governor, "In McKeesport, the un-American and unconstitutional regulation prevails that the sanction of the mayor must be had before public meetings can be held. It is impossible to hire a hall until this regulation is complied with."

Lysle denied the allegations, but he did little to change his ways. In July 1919, he gave permission for a local labor council, not the AFL, to meet at the "Slavish Hall" on White Street on the condition that the organizers submit a list of speakers and address the crowd in English only. The organizers balked and held a meeting on their own terms, bypassing the man Foster called "the petty Czar of McKeesport." By the end of their drive, they had tallied nearly four thousand new union members in the city.

HOMESTEAD

In Homestead, the site of the most violent steel strike to date, Burgess P.H. McGuire had little sympathy for the organizers and their flying squadron. A former steelworker and veteran of the 1892 strike, McGuire had since "made peace with the enemy," as Foster put it.

> [McGuire] *stated flatly that there would be no union meetings in Homestead, saying no halls could be secured. "But," said the organizers, "we have already engaged a hall." The next day the rent money was returned with the explanation that a mistake had been made....At first the Burgess, with a weather eye on McKeesport, did not molest* [public meetings]; *but when he saw the tremendous interest the steel workers showed and the rapidity with which they were joining the unions, he attempted to break up the meetings by arresting two of the organizers.*

In July 1919, Homestead police arrested Foster and another organizer at Eighth Avenue and McClure Street just as they prepared to address a crowd of hundreds. McGuire insisted he had only broken up the meeting because neighbors had complained about the noise and traffic, but organizers were skeptical. When the meetings drew attention from Homestead's immigrants, city officials—as in McKeesport—barred addresses in any language other than English.

Union men rejected the rule, noting that other organizations were free to carry on business in any language. Foster said that unions in Homestead "grew like beanstalks" in the months that followed.

MONESSEN AND THE "BOLSHEVIKI"

Monessen, a town far to the south in the Monongahela Valley, toward the coal and coke regions of Connellsville and West Virginia, represented a gateway to the Pittsburgh steel district. A miners' organizer named William P. Feeney spearheaded the efforts in Monessen from the outset, and he battled local officials as he sought to reserve halls and gain access to public spaces. "The Burgess of Monessen had flatly refused to allow him to hold any meetings in that town," Foster said. Among the pro-union voices was Mary Harris Jones, who was better known to her allies and to history as "Mother Jones." The Irish-born IWW organizer, who was already in her eighties by 1919, had joined the roving organizers and spent her time among the struggling immigrant workers surrounding Pittsburgh. "She had greater intimacy with the workers than anyone else in America. She is their 'Mother,'" Vorse wrote. "The foreign workers rarely meet Americans. The only Americans that some meet are bosses, landlords or tradesmen. Mother Jones is the only American woman that thousands of them have ever spoken to."

Jones and her allies had organized a fight against the Monessen government and had enlisted the help of miners in the surrounding towns by April 1919. The organizers and local newspapermen portrayed the fight in almost unrecognizably different terms. In Foster's telling, Jones and the AFL squadron brought ten thousand miners from the surrounding towns to march through Monessen, a move that drew massive public support and forced the burgess to relent. In local newspapers, they tell the story of a few hundred miners who marched briefly to celebrate the eight-hour day.

Undisputed, however, was the government's reaction to the organizing in the Monongahela Valley. On April 1, the day of the miners' protest march in Monessen, federal agents there arrested several suspected

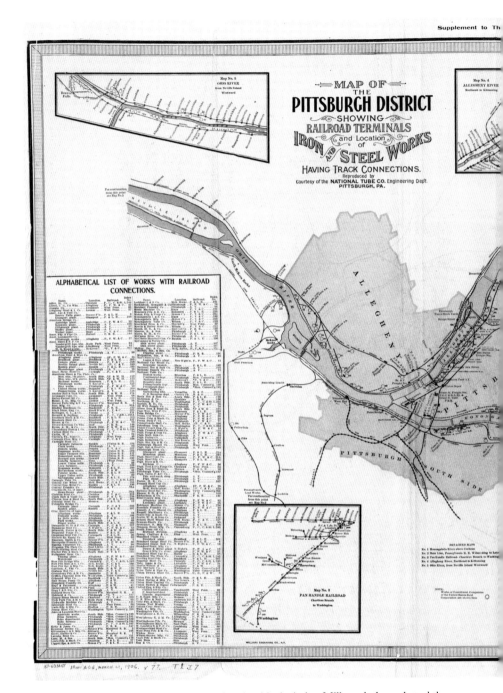

A railroad map shows U.S. Steel sites, rendered as black circles. Mills and plants dotted the valleys around Pittsburgh. *Library of Congress.*

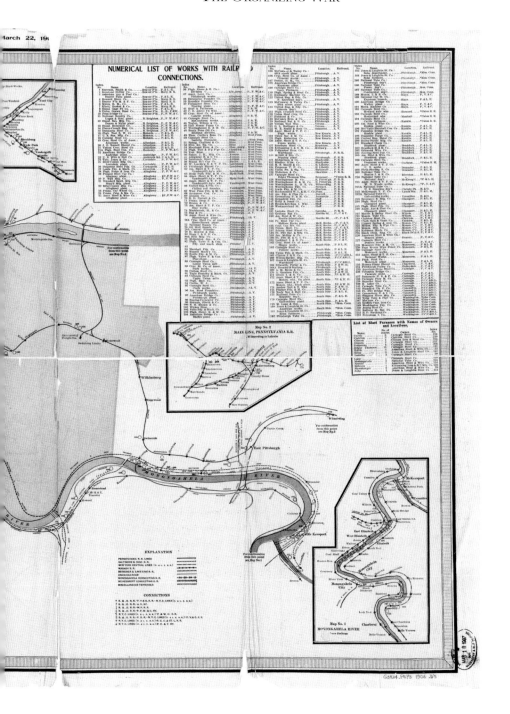

radical plotters who reporters described variously as "Soviet chiefs," "anarchists" and "Bolsheviki." It was a shocking, and indeed implausible, turn in the midst of an organizing drive. "Today the black flag of anarchy, surrounded by a color guard of men armed with automatic pistols to resist police interference would have been flung to the breeze during a parade and street demonstration in Monessen and Charleroi, had not the leaders been arrested yesterday," the *Pittsburgh Press* claimed. Police told reporters they had arrested as many as ten Russian-born radicals in Pittsburgh, Donora, Monessen and Bentleyville. Newspapers claimed, "The demonstration was to have been taken over by Bolshevists." The press also claimed that the demonstrators possessed maps of local Westinghouse facilities along with anarchist and IWW literature. The *Pittsburgh Post* offered the most shocking details:

> *The secret existence of a Pittsburgh soviet of Bolsheviki which had planned a demonstration under the black flag of anarchy today to initiate a general strike throughout the Monongahela valley was exposed yesterday by agents of the Federal department of justice who arrested five men alleged to be leaders. The soviet is declared to be conducted under the direction of Bolshevists of New York, who in turn are in direct communication with the Trotsky regime in Russia.*

The effect of the arrests was clear; in the steel valleys, immigrant workers who had already feared for their livelihoods now faced a new threat of armed agents breaking down their doors in the dead of night and dragging them off to prison and deportation. In her memoir, Mother Jones described a meeting she had with a worker's sobbing wife at her Monessen home:

> *"They have taken my man away and I do not know where they have taken him!"* Two little sobbing children clung to her gingham apron. Her tears fell on their little heads.
> *"I will find out for you. Tell me what happened."*
> *"Yesterday two men come. They open door; not knock. They come bust in. They say 'Your husband go back to Russia. He big Bolshevik!' I say, 'Who you?' They say, 'We big government United States. Big detect!' They open everything. They open trunks. They throw everything on floor. They take everything from old country. They say my husband never came back. They say my husband go Russia. Perhaps first they hang him up, they say."*

In Monessen, with a few serious claims and a handful of immigrants ready for deportation, local, state and federal officials had linked the steel organizing drive, however loosely, to a sudden fear of radical agitators. Things only got worse in the weeks following, when a series of bomb blasts shattered the remaining peace in Pittsburgh.

3

REVOLUTION IN THE AIR

It was a late Monday evening on June 2, 1919, and much of Pittsburgh was already asleep. A group of young men walked down Aylesboro Avenue in Squirrel Hill on the way home from a wedding in the upper-class neighborhood.

An explosion roared, blasting shrapnel into several homes. At 5437 Aylesboro Avenue, home of a high-ranking Pittsburgh Plate Glass official, B.J. Cassady, the front porch was blown to pieces, the house's entire front face was destroyed and the interior was wrecked. Next door, U.S. District Judge W.H.S. Thompson's home sustained several hundred dollars' worth of damage. Shrapnel and debris rocketed into nearby houses. The blast reportedly threw a baby into a pile of broken glass, where it somehow remained unharmed. Passersby rushed in to help, but no one was badly injured.

Moments later, but nearly seven miles away, in Sheraden, another explosion rocked the home of a railroad employee at 2633 Glasgow Street. The likely intended target was the man who lived across the street: W.W. Sibray. He was an immigration inspector who played a key role in deporting suspected radicals in western Pennsylvania. A neighbor said she saw a mysterious man planting a package in a porch vestibule at one of the homes but attached little importance to the sighting at the time.

Officials quickly realized the twin Allegheny County bombs were part of a much larger plot. Explosives had detonated nearly simultaneously in eight cities from Boston to Washington, D.C., and some used as much as twenty-five pounds of dynamite. The explosives targeted lawmakers, mayors and even the U.S. attorney general, Mitchell Palmer. At every site, including in Pittsburgh, they left a manifesto titled *Plain Words*. The *Pittsburgh Press* reprinted the leaflet, which read in part:

> *The powers that be make no secret of their will to stop here in America, the world-wide spread of revolution. The powers that be must reckon that they will have to accept the fight they have provoked. A time has come when the social question's solution can be delayed no longer; class war is on and cannot cease but with a complete victory for the international proletariat.*
>
> *The challenge is an old one, on "democratic" lords of the autocratic republic! We have been dreaming of freedom, we have talked of liberty. We have aspired to a better world and you jailed us, you clubbed us, you deported us, you murdered us whenever you could.*

The authorities moved swiftly on those they saw as the most likely suspects: the IWW. The radical union, which had already been penetrated by spies and undercover officers, shared the bombers' belief in unrelenting class war. Just twelve hours after the bombs exploded in Squirrel Hill and Sheraden, city police detectives raided the IWW offices at Moorhead Hall on Grant Street and at the Apollo Building on Fourth Avenue, just a short walk from the steel organizers' offices. According to news accounts, a detective was nearly killed when one bombing suspect, an Irish immigrant named John Johnson who was "internationally known as an agitator," fired a shot that grazed the officer's arm. Johnson was arrested, along with several other radicals.

Those who were accused of involvement hailed from many countries, including Hungary, Russia and Bulgaria, and police pointed to their radical literature as evidence of their involvement. Within days, however, their case against the Pittsburgh IWW began to falter. Investigators dropped the allegations one by one; reporters said Johnson declined to name any suspects or accomplices "despite quite severe handling." Johnson himself, a drifter who had worked in several states and had little history of violence, seemed an unlikely suspect for a well-organized nationwide bombing campaign. Before long, the authorities released all the Pittsburgh suspects, except for a handful who they deported as alien radicals.

In reality, it was unclear even to top investigators who precisely was behind the attacks. It was obviously a "Red Plot," as the *Gazette Times* put it, but which reds? IWW unionists or Bolshevik sympathizers seemed plausible suspects, as did the Italian anarchists who often sought revenge when their members were killed, deported or arrested. Indeed, one June 2 bomb suspect was tied to Italian militants. Carlo Valdinoci, who blew himself up while carrying out an attack in Washington, D.C., had edited the *Cronaca Sovversiva*, an Italian-language newspaper dedicated to the anarchist strategy of "propaganda of the deed." Investigators hinted at implausibly complex plots that involved German money funding Bolsheviks who in turn influenced Italian anarchists in America.

An early twentieth-century IWW poster. The militant "One Big Union" idea appealed to workers who were left out of traditional organizing structures. *Creator unidentified, via IWW.*

The difficulties that they had faced as they tried to pin down the true suspects highlighted the new reality: just as World War I had pushed Pittsburgh and its industry to new heights, it had also accelerated the radicalization of Pittsburgh's workers and immigrants. Police, federal agents and steel bosses no longer only had to contend with Amalgamated organizers and socialists stumping for election; they also had to contend with a constellation of new militant groups. Some of these groups were armed, and many took inspiration directly from war-torn Russia. How had they reached this point?

"One Big Union" Under Attack

Just as World War I had pushed the steel industry to new heights and spurred workers to organize by the thousands, the horror in Europe created new dangers and opportunities for Pittsburgh's far left. The Socialist Party gradually shrunk as the war ground on, particularly after the United States declared war in April 1917. Pennsylvania's Socialist Party chapters had around 9,800 dues-paying members in 1913; by 1918, they had just over 6,300. The party maintained an opposition to the war, which many socialists considered a pointless bloodbath that pitted worker against worker.

This antiwar stance was a dangerous one to take in an age of "one hundred percent Americanism." Patriotic marches and red-white-and-blue bunting seemed to be everywhere, and nationalist groups had taken to harassing immigrants who didn't appear sufficiently supportive of the war effort. President Woodrow Wilson's "Four Minute Men" addressed crowds with patriotic messages and encouraged them to join up and buy liberty bonds. Many of the antiwar socialists faced even greater danger as natives of the countries that America was fighting at the time—the German Empire and the Habsburg lands of Austria-Hungary. Youths from the North Side hurled snowballs at the International Socialist Lyceum and shouted, "Down with foreigners!" Men who mocked the war or who merely expressed doubts about their own involvement were liable to be targeted at work and home. Pro-war political figures and government investigators tended to conflate antiwar sentiment with pro-German espionage. Some even suggested that radical groups and unions, like the IWW, were directly funded by the government of Kaiser Wilhelm II. Postmaster General Albert Burleson refused to let his mail carriers deliver socialist magazines that opposed the war. In quiet conversations and private meetings, Pittsburgh socialists discussed methods of how to avoid the draft in order to avoid supporting what they considered an imperialist conflict.

In these conditions, it was little surprise that many of Pittsburgh's political leftists turned to even more radical organizations. In 1917, a group of IWW organizers met to rebuild the city's nearly defunct Wobbly movement and to gather the workers under the "One Big Union." The recent strikes at Westinghouse, in addition to ongoing IWW-led battles in Minnesota's iron ore mines, spurred organizers to consider a new drive of their own in the steel valleys.

Among these organizers was Jacob Margolis, who, in 1913, had appeared in the *Pittsburgh Press*'s "Socialist Bulletin" debating the merits of sabotage and direct action. As a longtime radical lawyer who had represented jailed socialists and union men in court, Margolis stood in the affirmative on the topics of sabotage and labor militancy. A curious figure, he was a relatively wealthy stock owner with expensive personal tastes. Margolis wasn't totally at home in either Pittsburgh's legal profession or its working-class movement. Nevertheless, he had become an important member of the city's far left wing, which clashed with moderate socialists who believed the revolution could be finished at the ballot box. Margolis publicly rejected violence and considered himself a pacifist, arguing that both "slowcialism" and armed revolution were inferior to organized workplace action. In an anarchist magazine called the *Mother Earth Bulletin*, which was edited by Emma Goldman and Frick's would-be assassin, Alexander

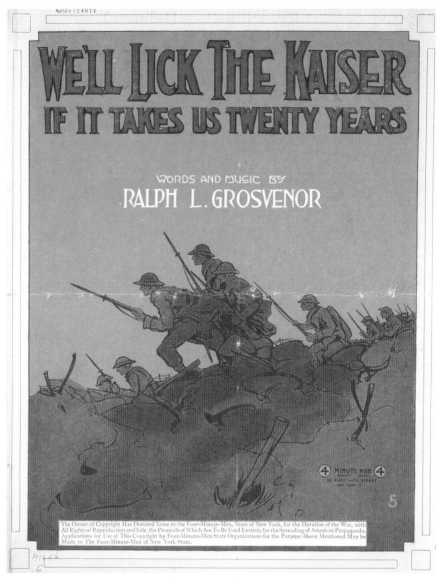

Patriotic sheet music calls for victory against "the Kaiser." European immigrants were often associated with enemy nations in the public eye. *Library of Congress.*

Berkman, Margolis wrote a mocking depiction of the trial of Walter Loan, a Wilkinsburg radical who had been accused of shooting a policeman:

> *Walter Loan, the Anarchist, does not bow reverently before the Prince of Death. He asks no mercy. He will live, suffer, work and go hungry to be himself.*
>
> *"The people with whom you associate are a menace to society," said the judge. Society, the painted courtesan—overfed, hypocritical, smug, propertied society. Indeed, thou art a menace to her ease and sloth, her property and security, Walter! Policemen have been shot before, and have, strange to relate, shot others, and yet the culprits hardly merited that exalted phrase, "menace to society." No, your crime was not the wounding of the policeman, but a shot at the rotten, filthy, parasitic, blood-drenched, enslaved society.*

Alongside Margolis in the IWW was Sam Scarlett, a Scottish immigrant who had organized workers in the Midwest before moving to Pittsburgh. Scarlett had traveled throughout Canada and the United States, and he had helped lead the Mesabi Range iron miners who joined a nationwide strike wave in 1916. Scarlett and his comrades argued that if the iron ore miners could be organized into the One Big Union, then so could the coal, coke and steel workers. Scarlett even traveled to Ohio, where he recruited workers for the IWW and urged them to move east and take steel jobs in Pittsburgh. Joining Scarlett and Margolis was Jack Law, a Pittsburgh-born IWW man who had worked on the other side of the country before settling to organize in his hometown. Law, a loose cannon who had been in trouble with his fellow IWW members in the past, was inspired to renew his commitment to the cause in Pittsburgh, as historian Charles H. McCormick noted when studying Law's letters to his comrades. In them, Law writes, "[My plan] is to cooperate with anybody or try alone to get the neuculis [*sic*] of an organization together starting in the coke regions & working toward Pittsburgh....[If we] get the coke workers we will have a powerful club over the mill-men owing to the fact that we have the raw material from both ends."

This cluster of organizers quickly set to work in Pittsburgh in 1917. In beer-fueled meetings and speaking events with fellow radicals, they detailed their plan to organize the iron, coke and coal workers to encircle and conquer the steel trust. Scarlett discussed it with the Minnesota miners:

We had beat the Steel Trust to the point of raw material....I was going to Pittsburgh to the point of production of finished products [to] *organize and beat the Steel Trust again and I asked them if when that time came they would stick and strike at the mines so that the Steel Trust would be completely tied up. They answered yes POSITIVELY.*

Although they had only a handful of Pittsburgh workers actively on their side—fewer than twenty at their first meetings—the Wobblies were laying the groundwork for an organizing campaign of their own, just months before Foster and the AFL would launch theirs on a massive scale.

All of this work did not go unnoticed by the authorities; federal and local governments spent the war years accelerating their efforts against suspected German spies, labor radicals and draft-dodgers. By 1917, the Bureau of Investigation, predecessor to the FBI, had set up a "Radical Squad" in Pittsburgh. With just a handful of agents at its height, the squad recruited confidential informants and labor spies alongside private agents and members of the navy's Military Intelligence Directorate.

Perhaps their most important spy, as detailed by the historian McCormick, was Louis "Leo" Wendell, who was better known by his undercover alias, Walsh. Wendell's background was mysterious, although he may have been involved in military intelligence before his sudden arrival in Pittsburgh. Wendell's federal handlers waited as he introduced himself and carefully planted cover stories in Pittsburgh's radical circles throughout 1917. An article in the *Pittsburgh Press* described him as a "nationally known radical" who had been "watched closely by government agents for over a year." Few readers could suspect how true the latter statement would turn out to be. Wendell's first mission was to disrupt the People's Council of America for Peace and Democracy, which was a broad front that opposed the war that suffered heavily from police repression and government investigation. Wendell was present in the earliest days of the city's reformed IWW chapter, attending its charter meetings and working to forge connections with other radical and left-wing groups across the city. He kept meticulous records of his interactions with fellow radicals, and he wrote frequently to his bosses. Wendell was not only spying on the IWW and its antiwar allies, he was also attempting to take control of these groups and destroy them from within.

By summer 1917, the assault on the IWW was ready. Federal officials across the country, including those who were in the union's base of operations in Chicago, planned a simultaneous attack to break the IWW's back and

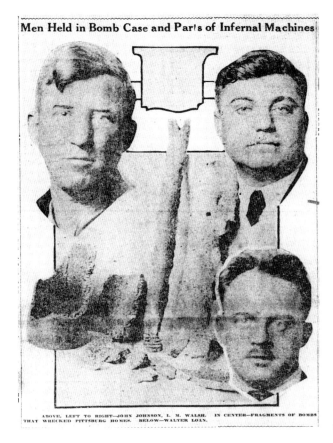

Men Held in Bomb Case and Parts of Infernal Machines

ABOVE, LEFT TO RIGHT—JOHN JOHNSON, L. M. WALSH. IN CENTER—FRAGMENTS OF BOMBS THAT WRECKED PITTSBURG HOMES. BELOW—WALTER LOAN.

A 1919 *Pittsburgh Press* composite shows local IWW suspects in a nationwide wave of radical bombings. "L.M. Walsh," *top right*, was actually an undercover agent. Pittsburgh Press *via Newspapers.com.*

imprison its key figures. Officials asked the Pittsburgh Radical Squad to submit the names of known local members, which were presumably gathered by Wendell under his false identity.

On September 5, 1917, police raided the Wobbly offices in nearly every city where the union operated. In Pittsburgh, investigators opened the door of the "Radical Library" in the McGeagh building downtown and ransacked the office, looking for radical literature and connections to German intelligence. Inside, they collected magazines, pamphlets and fundraising materials, along with newspapers they snatched from a nearby vendor. They found no evidence of foreign ties, but the local press hyped the raids as a possible step in stopping an antiwar conspiracy. As the *Pittsburgh Press* reported a day after the McGeagh raid:

> *The raids on the newsstands attracted the attention of many persons on the street and crowds collected when dealers protested against the removal*

of the literature from their stands. This literature, with that taken from the office of the "Radical Library," will be forwarded to Chicago....There is no regular I.W.W. headquarters in Pittsburgh, it is said, and the warrants were against individuals, who are known to be active in the interest of the organization. They are, according to Government officers, the same people who have been taking active part in all anti-war activities in Pittsburgh.

Not long after the raids, a grand jury filed charges against scores of Wobbly activists nationwide, including several with Pittsburgh connections. The assault led to new allegations in the following months, some of which tied labor radicals to foreign influence. In mid-November 1917, federal investigators and marshals carried out another Pittsburgh raid; this one was against the Hungarian branch of the Pittsburgh Wobblies. The group, which included many immigrants and German-speaking members, raised fears of "seditious propaganda against the United States" from radicals tied to America's wartime enemy. Officers carried out simultaneous raids across the North Side of Pittsburgh; one raid took place at 805 East Street, which was the location of the group's headquarters (it is home to a Croatian cultural society today), and another took place at two North Side homes where the group's officers lived. "Red flags and a number of group pictures found in the room were seized," the *Daily Post* reported. "The organization, it is said, was formed some months ago by members of the German-Hungarian Beneficial Union of the Northside and the meetings were held in the beneficial society's hall."

Raids, arrests and growing fears of government informants wore down many Pittsburgh radicals, and some groups shrunk or folded entirely as the war dragged on. Indeed, Wendell reported months after the North Side raids that the Hungarian IWW had been battered into submission. Still, the immigrant groups that occupied a growing share of Pittsburgh's radical left, and that composed most of the steel mill's workforce, remained defiant. McCormick cites in his book, *Seeing Reds*, Frieda Truhar, a Pittsburgher from a radical family of Croatian descent. Truhar said police questioned her parents about their radical and antiwar statements, but that didn't stop her father from participating in antiwar activities. "The socialist Croatians in Pittsburgh continued to push antiwar leaflets printed in English through letter slots," she said.

As the war ground on and the police turned the screws on socialist organizations, radicals hailing from eastern and southern Europe found inspiration in an unlikely place closer to their homelands: the Russian Empire.

"A Capitalist's Heaven and a Workman's Hell"

Russia and its possessions, including Finland, Poland and the Ukraine, were originally home to thousands of the poor, often non-English-speaking workers who mined coke and coal and poured steel in Pittsburgh and the surrounding river valleys. Millions of Russians died on the side of the Allies during World War I, fighting under an autocratic tsar whose grip over the country was quickly slipping. In 1917, bread riots and strikes broke out in open chaos in the nation's royal capital, Petrograd (also known as St. Petersburg). Joined by disaffected soldiers and sailors, the strikers overthrew Tsar Nicholas II and established a new provisional government to rule in his stead.

American socialists and labor organizers watched with interest as Russia, which was often dismissed as a backward, peasant country, became ground zero for a globally revolutionary movement. The provisional government under liberal Alexander Kerensky failed to carry out the reforms that workers, peasants and political radicals had demanded. Worst of all, Kerensky tried to continue to fight in the murderous war against Germany and Austria-Hungary despite mass protest. Radical socialists, and most notably the Bolshevik faction led by the exiled Vladimir Lenin, organized units of armed workers and formed parallel government structures in Russia's largest cities. These councils, called soviets, called to mind the revolutionary communes of France that, decades earlier, had inspired American radicals to action. For months, clashes and political battles flared as the Bolsheviks clawed for control of local governments and threatened Kerensky's power.

In November (October by the contemporary Russian reckoning), Lenin and his allies launched an all-out revolt against the provisional government. Armed workers and mutinous soldiers surged into the palaces of government and declared control over Petrograd and Moscow. Their armies joined in open battle against the remaining government loyalists while their diplomats sought a separate peace with Germany and its allies.

In the United States, as exemplified in the Pittsburgh newspapers, the Bolsheviks inspired a mix of fascination and terror. The radicals, waving red banners and calling for the overthrow of capitalism in every country, were an unfamiliar sight to steel bosses and politicians who had lived for years in relative peace with their laborers. The *Pittsburgh Gazette Times* denounced "Bolsheviki arrogance" and said that "plain speaking people will have no difficulty in describing what kind of fools the Bolsheviki are." But to American radicals, like those in the IWW, the Bolsheviks were the vanguard of a new order. The famed left-wing journalist John Reed celebrated the "ten days that shook the world" in Petrograd, while in Pittsburgh, Yiddish-speaking artists performed a play on "the New Russia."

World War I ended with an Allied victory on November 11, 1918, despite the withdrawal of the newly formed Russian Soviet Federative Socialist Republic and its allies. While Pittsburgh newspapers marked "WILD PEACE CELEBRATIONS," the Bolsheviks were fighting for their lives in Russia. The world's largest country was embroiled in a civil war, with alliances shifting between factions of socialists ("Reds"), monarchists and capitalists ("Whites") and a collection of anarchists and Islamic and nationalist groups. The Bolsheviks under Lenin renamed themselves the Russian Communist Party and, in doing so, drew a direct line between themselves, Karl Marx and even the French Revolution of the eighteenth century, where the term "communist" was first coined. To American radicals who rejected the old paths to power, communism would become a new guiding light.

In Pittsburgh and Pennsylvania at large, the revolution would reopen wounds that dated back to 1913, when Allegheny County's socialists split in a fight between the slow-moving approach of electoralism and the fiery, "direct action" approach of the IWW. This conflict set the stage for a far more vicious battle in the years to come, and news of violent reprisals and authoritarian policies in Russia only made matters worse. The Russian communists made no bones about the need for extreme methods; Lenin himself argued that a single ruling party had to enforce control to stop counterrevolution. Leon Trotsky, commander of the Red Army, also defended his methods in the book *Terrorism and Communism*. This didn't sit well with the American "slowcialists" who advocated for a peaceful transition to power.

By early 1919, communism was undeniably on the rise. The Reds were on the verge of victory in Russia, a Bolshevik force had seized power in Hungary and so-called Spartacists were fighting in the streets and declaring Soviet republics in defeated Germany. The Socialist Party of America, which still counted thousands of Pennsylvania members, was fraying at the seams in a battle between its so-called left and right wings. In several cities, radicals who looked favorably upon Russia had taken control of their local party organizations. They established new magazines and newspapers— the *Class Struggle*, the *Internationalist*, the *Voice of Labor*—and called on their party to join the newly forming Communist International. In Pennsylvania, the battle was met swiftly by those in charge just weeks before the party was set to meet for an emergency convention. When many of the left-wing

Philadelphia members refused to follow their superiors' commands, they were purged from the party, and their branches were reformed only by the members who agreed to take a loyalty oath: "I am not and have not been a member of the so-called Left Wing." Even Pittsburgh newspapers mocked the split. An editorial item in the *Post* noted threateningly, "A socialist 'left wing' has appeared in New York. In time there will be a grand clipping of the wings of all the disturbers in this country."

The summer of 1919 would be a fateful time for labor radicals in Pittsburgh and throughout the United States. As the Socialist Party gathered for its emergency convention in early September, two factions were actively splitting from its ranks to form a new, militant movement. Some, mainly those involved in immigrant "foreign language federations," sought a clean break to form a new political party. Others, including the journalist John Reed, wanted a last chance to win over their fellow Socialists before they departed. In the end, their efforts failed, and their comrades were ejected from the Socialist Party. The United States was now home to not one, but two openly communist political organizations. One was led largely by American-born activists, and the other was led by immigrant workers and their language federations. The split could be felt in Pittsburgh and its neighboring towns, where federal agents reported angry speeches by immigrant socialists who demanded a new party.

The immigrant group, the Communist Party of America, met in Chicago for its founding convention. Among its branches were the Pittsburgh Council of Workers' Delegates, a group with 1,000 members led by the Lithuanian-born radical Juozas Baltrušaitis. In Monessen, another Lithuanian, Anthony Bankauskas, led a 180-member chapter of Lithuanians and Ukrainians. Their comrades and temporary rivals, the Communist Labor Party, formed at about the same time, and both quickly sought recognition from Lenin's Soviet government. It wasn't long before the new Communist International, the Comintern, extended a membership invitation to the IWW as well. Investigators reported small Communist branches forming around the city; some were already planning meetings at the International Socialist Lyceum on the North Side.

Pittsburgh was now host to at least three organizations that openly affiliated themselves with the new Russian government, a prospect that terrified both businessmen and Red Squad investigators in Pittsburgh. Smaller groups, like the so-called Soldiers and Sailors Soviet, dotted the city and gathered in meeting halls. The radicals were hardened by years of repression, dedicated to their cause and guided—spiritually, at least—

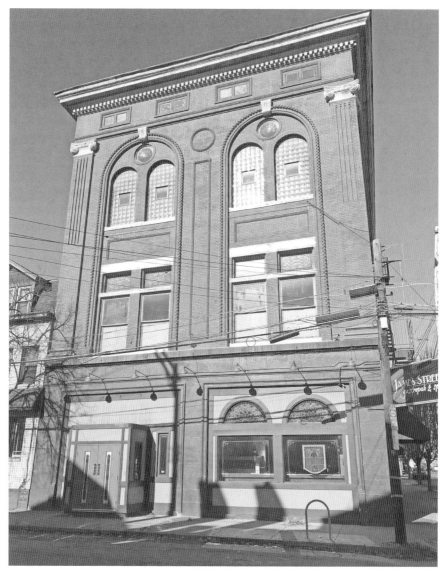

The building at the corner of James and Foreland Streets was once called the International Socialist Lyceum. From 1918 to about 1940, the building housed socialist and communist groups. *By the author.*

by a foreign government that hoped to extend the communist revolution around the world. A Socialist and committee member by the name of Stankowitz, who was an industrial worker from Pittsburgh, described his hopes in a letter to Reed, just weeks after the string of bombings that hit Pittsburgh and months after the "Soviet chiefs" were arrested in the Monessen Valley. "Whatever happens, our future propaganda should be in factories, mines, mills, etc.," Stankowitz wrote. "If the Communist Party does not unite with radical industrial unions, she will be a failure."

Their interest in the steel mills and coal mines of western Pennsylvania was genuine, and it spurred discussion even in the halls of power in Moscow and Petrograd. When the U.S. Senate called for a series of sensational hearings on "Bolshevik propaganda," the economic theorist Raymond Robins testified to the passion with which returning Russian immigrants discussed American life:

> *There returned to Russia immediately at the beginning of the revolution great numbers of Russians from America, immigrants, both Gentile and Jew....They represented genuine, honest men, who had met America at America's worst—and America's worst, when we are honest and frank with ourselves, is evil. I know that and you know that....Men came back to Russia and spoke of the steel mills of Pennsylvania, spoke of the twelve-hour day, spoke of the twenty-four-hour shifts every two weeks, spoke of the seven-day weeks, spoke of those things of the nonunion coal mines of West Virginia, of the tenement sweatshops, of the political system of our great cities, and the political police court with its corruption; interpreted America as being a capitalist's heaven and a workman's hell.*

As Robins spoke, organizers in Pittsburgh were preparing for their final attack that they hoped would end those very conditions.

4

PREPARING FOR BATTLE

To many of the national steel organizers, the workers were becoming too militant, too quickly. The free-speech campaigns in the Monongahela Valley were yielding fruit, and organizing operations in other cities had already drawn tens of thousands of workers to the union cause. Telegrams and letters poured in every day from field workers, warning that local strikes could break out if the members' power wasn't properly harnessed. Foster wrote, "So bad was the situation by early spring that, lacking other means of relief, local strikes were threatening all over the country. To allow these forlorn-hope walkouts to occur would have meant disintegration and disaster to the whole campaign. They had to be checked at all costs and the movement kept upon a national basis."

The solution, the National Committee decided, was to hold mass meetings at the Labor Temple at the corner of Washington Street and Webster Avenue. On May 25, 1919—with the free-speech battles around Pittsburgh in full swing—583 representatives from across the country gathered to hear updates and debate their next moves. Foster said the objective was "to demonstrate to the rank and file how fast the national movement was developing, to turn their attention to it strongly, and thus hearten them to bear their hardships until it could come to their assistance." But privately, organizers spoke more frankly. They planned to "hold the men in line better and to make them wait more patiently."

The steelworkers didn't want to wait patiently. Over concerns from AFL officials, the Pittsburgh delegates passed a resolution demanding collective bargaining with the steel companies.

It be the will of this conference that a joint effort be made by all unions affiliated with the National Committee for Organizing Iron and Steel Workers to enter into negotiations with the various steel companies to the end that better wages, shorter hours, improved working conditions and the trade-union system of collective bargaining be established in the steel industry.

Their vote came amid a tense back-and-forth with the steel bosses. In a letter sent days before the delegates met in Pittsburgh, Gary—the serious-minded, teetotaling head of U.S. Steel—flatly rejected union recognition. The steel magnates may have been prepared to negotiate shorter hours, better pay or days off, but they would not tolerate total union power in their mills. Gary told M.F. Tighe, president of the Amalgamated:

I agree that it is the patriotic duty of all good citizens to use their efforts in stemming the tide of unrest in the industrial world whenever and wherever it exists. As you know, we do not confer, negotiate with, or combat labor unions as such. We stand for the open shop, which permits a man to engage in the different lines of employment, whether he belongs to a labor union or not. We think this attitude secures the best results to the employees generally and to the employers. In our way, and in accordance with our best judgment, we are rendering efficient patriotic service in the direction indicated by you.

Weeks passed, and the organizing campaign continued. Gary received a new letter in June, not from Tighe or a steel representative, but from Samuel Gompers. As the head of the AFL, Gompers was politically moderate and opposed to radical unions, and he appealed to the steel bosses' fear of revolution. The organizing drive wasn't a rebellion, he said, and it would suit both sides to sit down at the negotiating table.

A campaign of organization was begun in June, 1918, and within that period we have secured the organization of more than one hundred thousand of the employees in the iron and steel industry. The prospects for the complete organization are, I am informed, exceedingly bright. Of course, knowing the police of the Organized Labor movement I have the honor in part to represent, we aim to accomplish the purposes of our labor movement; that is, better conditions for the toilers, by American methods, and American understandings, not by revolutionary methods or the inauguration of a cataclysm. We believe in the effort of employer and employees to sit around a table, and meeting thus, face to face, and having a better understanding of the other's position[.]

William Z. Foster, *center*, during or around the time of the steel strike. Foster's radical writings became the subject of nationwide controversy. *Library of Congress.*

There was no answer. "To Mr. Gompers' courteous letter, Czar Gary did not deign to reply," Foster wrote. "This was bad. It looked like war." Across Pennsylvania and Ohio, workers were threatening to go it alone. In Johnstown, a workers' council announced that it would strike immediately if a plan wasn't put in place; Foster told his superiors, "Great strikes are threatening."

On July 20, 1919, exactly a month after Gompers sent his unanswered letter, the National Committee met again at the Pittsburgh Labor Temple. Representatives from the dozens of participating unions issued a new resolution; a strike vote was to be held nationwide, and they sought authorization to walk out of the mills if their demands were not met. Along with the strike vote was a list of twelve demands, which was to be submitted to Gary and his fellow steel bosses:

- *Right of collective bargaining*
- *Reinstatement of all men discharged for union activities with pay for time lost*
- *Eight-hour day*
- *One day's rest in seven*
- *Abolition of twenty-four-hour shift*
- *Increases in wages sufficient to guarantee American standard of living*
- *Standard scales of wages in all trades and classifications of workers*
- *Double rates of pay for all overtime after eight hours, holiday and Sunday work*
- *Check-off system of collecting union dues and assessments*
- *Principles of seniority to apply in the maintenance, reduction and increase of working forces*
- *Abolition of company unions*
- *Abolition of physical examination of applicants for employment*

These twelve demands would become the basis for the workers' coming battle; many of them, including the end of full-day shifts, true eight-hour days and days off, had been hotly contested for years. Now, tens of thousands of steelworkers nationwide were united in demanding them.

Each participating union circulated strike ballots by the thousands that said, "The Union Committees are now seeking to get higher wages, shorter hours and better working conditions from the steel companies. Are you willing to back them up to the extent of stopping work should the companies refuse to concede these demands?" These ballots, which were circulated from Foster's office in the Magee building, detailed the demands in six languages: "BALLOT—TAJNO GLASANJE—SZAVAZZON—VOTAZIONE—HLASOVACI LISTOK—BALOT."

The balloting would take a month, which allowed precious time for the organizers to extend their efforts in less militant areas. While the organizers had achieved tremendous success in other states and in a few outlying towns, Pittsburgh and the Monongahela Valley remained difficult. Still, Foster wrote, "Enthusiasm was intense….Whole districts voted in the affirmative. Of all the thousands of ballots cast in Homestead, Braddock, Rankin, McKeesport, Vandergrift, Pittsburgh and Monessen not one was in the negative. Donora produced one 'no' vote." The final tally, organizers claimed, was 98 percent in favor of a strike.

Organizers gave Gary just a few days to answer their demands. When Foster and two fellow union leaders arrived in Gary's New York office, they were turned away. Their only reply came in the form of a letter, dated August 27, that repeated earlier rejections nearly word-for-word:

> *We do not think you are authorized to represent the sentiment of a majority of the employees of the United States Steel Corporation and its subsidiaries....As heretofore publicly stated and repeated, our Corporation and subsidiaries, although they do not combat labor unions as such, decline to discuss business with them. The Corporation and subsidiaries are opposed to the "closed shop." They stand for the "open shop," which permits one to engage in any line of employment whether one does or does not belong to a labor union.*

The two sides were at an impasse. Only one option was available to the union men before they would launch a strike, which was scheduled for September 22 if nothing changed.

The organizers sought help from President Woodrow Wilson, who had come to their aid when overwork and anti-union sentiment threatened production at the height of World War I. The war was over, however, and Wilson was traveling Europe to promote the League of Nations. A steel strike could throw Wilson's plans out of order and force his attention homeward just as he was hoping to extend American influence overseas. The president privately expressed sympathy with the union men and sought counsel with Gary, but he had little success.

On September 11, the organizers opened the Pittsburgh newspapers with a shock. "WILSON URGES STEEL MEN TO DELAY STRIKE," the *Gazette Times* said. The president had sent a telegram to union leaders urging "the wisdom and advisability of postponing action of any kind until after the forthcoming industrial conference in Washington." The president's move was a grave miscalculation, the organizers feared. There could be no delay—the steel bosses were bracing for a strike, and supporters were already being fired en masse. Foster wrote:

> *Conditions in the steel industry were desperate. Everywhere the employers were making vigorous attacks on the unions. From Chicago, Wheeling, Buffalo, Pittsburgh, and many other points large numbers of men were being thrown out of work because of their union membership. Johnstown was a bleeding wound. In the towns along the Monongahela River thousands of discharged men walked the streets, and their number was daily being heavily increased.*

A postwar poster by artist Gerrit Beneker calls for labor peace as soldiers returned home from Europe. *Library of Congress.*

The threatened strike was making headlines everywhere. The business pages of the *Pittsburgh Press* warned of sliding stocks: "Threat of a steel strike by September 22 threw a scare into Wall Street today and the market was demoralized at today's opening." The possible steel strike wasn't the only havoc dominating the newspapers. In Pittsburgh, readers learned that vigilante snipers were prepared to fire on striking "foreign-born employees" at an Indiana railcar factory, and in Boston, the police were on strike, which led to mass riots and the activation of militia troops. Still, Gary balked; he told Wilson he had evidence that 85 percent of U.S. Steel workers would remain on the job.

Officials around Pittsburgh prepared for the inevitable. Sheriff William S. Haddock issued an order that illegal public gatherings would be met with force, and he called on all mayors and burgesses to aid his forces in stopping potential violence. "Sheriff Haddock deputized five thousand men," said Vorse, the British journalist. "He said that there were only five thousand people striking in the Pittsburg district. He deputized one man for every striker." Organizers argued that the true number of deputies was far higher, perhaps in the tens of thousands. Even as steel bosses breezily dismissed the threat of walkouts in the Pittsburgh newspapers, they prepared for violence. Officials told the *Pittsburgh Post*:

> *Notwithstanding reports to the contrary, the mills of the United States Steel Corporation have not made extraordinary plans to combat the strike. The number of our men who will respond to the strike call will be negligible and will not have an appreciable effect on our operations. We are not looking for trouble, but if it comes, then something will be done to protect our loyal workmen and our property.*

The *New York World* noted on the planned strike date:

> *In the Pittsburgh district thousands of deputy sheriffs have been recruited at several of the larger plants. The Pennsylvania State Constabulary has been concentrated at commanding points. At other places the authorities have organized bodies of war veterans as special officers....It is as though preparations were made for actual war.*

Foster dismissed the gathering police forces and government agencies as "lackey officials...hardly more than public service departments of the steel trust." Haddock's riot proclamation, he said, was tantamount to a

Heavily armed policemen guard a mill in Farrell. The Shenango Valley was the scene of brutal fighting, which included reported snipers. *Library of Congress.*

declaration of martial law throughout Allegheny County. Mounted police soon crashed through a public meeting of workers in North Clairton, and others rode into a gathering at Glassport "in true Cossack fashion." The city papers were packed with messages against the impending strike that either downplayed its importance or warned of mass violence and havoc. As September 22 approached, the press raised fears of immigrant violence and "aliens" stirring up chaos while American-born workers remained loyal. "It is the belief of the steel operators in the Pittsburgh district that if there is any trouble at all it will be confined to those mills where the foreign element is in the majority," said the *Pittsburgh Post.* "About seventy-five percent of the workmen of this concern are said to be foreigners."

Despite all this, thousands of workers were prepared to walk off. Some two hundred thousand copies of a strike notice were distributed at mills across the country, which read:

STRIKE SEPTEMBER 22, 1919

The workers in the iron and steel mills and blast furnaces, not working under union agreements, are requested not to go to work on September 22, and to refuse to resume their employment until such time as the demands of the organizations have been conceded by the steel corporations.

The union committees have tried to arrange conferences with the heads of the steel companies in order that they might present our legitimate demands for the right of collective bargaining, higher wages, shorter hours and better working conditions. But the employers have steadfastly refused to meet them. It therefore becomes our duty to support the committees' claims, in accordance with the practically unanimous strike vote, by refusing to work in the mills on or after September 22, until such time as our just demands have been granted. And in our stoppage of work let there be no violence. The American Federation of Labor has won all its great progress by peaceful and legal methods.

IRON AND STEEL WORKERS! A historic decision confronts us. If we will but stand together now like men our demands will soon be granted and a golden era of prosperity will open for us in the steel industry. But if we falter and fail to act this great effort will be lost, and we will sink back into a miserable and hopeless serfdom. The welfare of our wives and children is at stake. Now is the time to insist upon your rights as human beings.

STOP WORK SEPTEMBER 22

5

AMERICA'S GREAT INDUSTRIAL WAR

The morning of Monday, September 22, 1919, broke to silence at steel mills across the United States. Workers walked off, stayed home and rallied with their union allies from Chicago, Pittsburgh and Johnstown, totally shutting down mills in many of the outlying cities. "On September 22 they struck throughout the entire industry with a discipline and universality that will be remembered as long as steel is made in America.…The shutdown was almost complete," Foster wrote. "Throughout the country, the industry was stricken by paralysis. On average, the strike was at least ninety percent effective." However, in Pittsburgh, where the campaign had been met with brutal violence, it was feared that fewer workers would turn out.

In the early hours of the strike, newspapers seemed unwilling or unable to fully estimate the workers' response. As reports trickled in from outlying plants, it appeared thousands had struck, but the question remained: would the Pittsburgh plants remain open? The *Pittsburgh Press* reported on the first day, "Late reports failed to show whether the walk out will develop into America's greatest industrial war." And the *Daily Post* said, "At seven o'clock this morning the strike order of the steel workers' union goes into effect, but no one was seer enough yesterday to venture a prediction as to the number who will answer it." Union officers had carried out eleventh-hour meetings to gauge support from their locals.

The first hours did not bode well for a peaceful resolution, however. In North Clairton, police charged a crowd of hundreds of strikers, who the newspapers noted were "mostly foreigners," amid an exchange of blows and gunfire. The strikers had allegedly threatened men who had dared to appear at the Clairton works; the battle grew until mounted officers beat and arrested several strikers. The strikers' names show the immigrant makeup of the strike's first days: Hodak, Torvich and Kabonich, among others. In McKeesport, gunshots could be heard as police clashed with massed workers and their allies. Foster wrote:

> *Pittsburgh was the storm center. There, in its stronghold, the Steel Trust went ahead with strike-breaking measures unprecedented in industrial history. It provisioned and fortified its great mills and furnaces, surrounding them with stockades topped off with heavily charged electric wires, and bristling with machine guns.*

While the authorities prepared for war, the newspapers—uncertain as they were about the strike's scale—soon threw cold water on the workers' claims. In an era when firsthand accounts traveled by word of mouth and newspaper stories were rushed across the country instantaneously by wire,

A strike leader addresses a crowd of workers in Gary, Indiana. The city was eventually subjected to martial law. *Library of Congress.*

Crowds of strikers and sympathizers gather to hear a speech. Authorities often broke up strike meetings by force. *Library of Congress.*

the mill owners' claims often came out on top. "The steel companies' most powerful weapon was creating and fostering the feeling that 'it's a fizzle, we're making steel, the strike's all over,'" researchers from the Interchurch World Movement said in a 1920 report. Where the organizers assured the workers that the steel trust could be beaten, the mill owners sought to prove that they couldn't. The first articles in the local press underscored that attitude. The *Pittsburgh Press* ran a single column, listing the organizers' claims side-by-side with those of the bosses. In Pittsburgh, the *Press* reported, "The police said that but [a] few workers struck. Union officials claimed large numbers of the men walked out." Almost every town and plant reported that it was working at full capacity, or nearly full, with only "the foreign element" heeding the strike call. The papers were hardly neutral; the unions, the *Press* reported on the front page, had challenged U.S. Steel "determined to break its marvelous independence." A later analysis would find that the newspapers' repeated claims of victory tallied a total of 4.8 million workers who had returned to the mills—many times the number of steelworkers in the entire country!

The strike organizers clearly felt they had succeeded, at least in the first days. Foster's estimates were massive: twenty-five thousand men struck in Pittsburgh, nine thousand in Homestead and ten thousand in Braddock. He also claimed that the steel valley around Youngstown tallied some seventy thousand workers on strike. In Chicago, it was reported that "when the pent-up force was finally released it swept the district like a flood, leaving hardly a wheel turning anywhere."

JOHNSTOWN

Few districts struck more completely than Johnstown, the steel valley surrounded by Cambria County's coal mines. Even the Pittsburgh newspapers quickly acknowledged that the plants of the Cambria Steel Co. had been silenced. The months-long battle over union representation, which saw the bosses' company union effectively driven out and the workers organized by the thousands, had clearly had an effect. Foster was exuberant: "In Johnstown, the Cambria Company was so hard hit that, swallowing its pride, it had to ask the hated unions for a detachment of workers to protect its plants." Vorse, the British journalist crisscrossing the steel country, described the silence around the once-powerful Johnstown mills.

> *The Cambria Steel Company is the core of the town. From the railway station, I looked down into the yards. Rust was over all. Piles of scrap covered with rust, mounds of billets covered with rust, car-loads of pig iron covered with rust. Paint scaling from black chimneys. Rust crawling up chimneys. In this yard, nothing stirred. There was no sign of life.*
>
> *A man walked slowly through the empty yard. It was startling to see anything move through that quiet place, through the mounds of iron on which rust had fallen like a red snow. It seemed the graveyard of industry. Johnstown's men had left the mills in rust and silence....Up and down walked groups of idle steel workers, big men drifting on the slack tide of idleness into the hall of their headquarters. Cambria Steel shut down.*

Only the bosses and white-collar clerks dared enter the mills there, investigators reported. The company made no effort to reopen the mills, and the city government maintained a general air of neutrality. Workers there picketed freely and held four meetings every night. When a company guard ordered the picketing men to leave, a city policeman took the side of the workers and told them to continue.

THE "BLACK VALLEY"

The Allegheny Valley above Pittsburgh had seen some horrific violence in the weeks before the strike. It was there that Fannie Sellins, the beloved mine organizer, had been shot dead by deputies, and it was there that unions had historically faced some of their toughest odds. On the strike's first day, the local newspapers claimed that most of the men would swiftly return to work. "Sixty percent of the more than five thousand employees of the Allegheny and West Penn Steel companies at Brackenridge are expected to report for work at eight o'clock this morning," the *Daily Post* said. "Officials at both companies last night declared that no difficulty was anticipated in operating mills today because the vote of the men Saturday showed they would return in large numbers."

Nevertheless, reporters acknowledged that the Allegheny Valley plants were operating well below capacity. Many workers picked up their tools and clothes after their final strike meeting and refused to return; others finished the morning's work before launching their walkoff. "Federation workers were busy in Natrona yesterday, where seventy-five percent of the foreign-speaking laborers who have signed cards live," the *Post* said. From the organizers' new Natrona office, union men warned the workers against violence. Placards appeared in Tarentum, Brackenridge and Natrona that said, "Iron and Steel Workers—STRIKE—Don't Be Scabs." The effect was powerful. In contrast to the bosses, who said most departments would remain open, Foster tallied at least a 90 percent turnout throughout the so-called Black Valley.

THE MONONGAHELA

"In the Monongahela river section, it was not so good," Foster admitted. He claimed that seemingly every worker joined the fight in Donora and Monessen, but elsewhere, whether by ineffective organizing or the workers' opposition to the threat of official violence, the lights stayed on in the Monongahela Valley mills. It was reported, "Due to the terrorism prevailing, exact figures were almost impossible to get for the other

Constables strike a bystander, alleged to be Rudolph Dressel of Homestead, while clearing the street in September 1919. *United Electrical Workers via Historic Pittsburgh.*

towns." Nevertheless, organizers claimed that the overwhelming majority of steelworkers had walked off in Clairton, Braddock and Rankin. In McKeesport and Duquesne, the results were less effective.

Most of the mills in McKeesport remained open, the newspapers proclaimed. "There were unusually large numbers of foreigners on the streets of McKeesport today, but they were orderly," said the *Press*. Thousands of newly minted deputies roamed the town and waited for violence to break out.

The Jones and Laughlin plant on the South Side remained open; the disheartened workers there had failed in an independent strike action two years earlier. "Little disorder had been reported from McKeesport, Clairton, Homestead, Braddock, Duquesne or other nearby points, after the walkout order went into effect," the *Press* claimed. State police troopers stood at the mill gates.

In North Braddock, mill police reported an exchange of gunfire with two men who had allegedly tried to break into a plant superintendent's home. The "thugs" fled the scene.

The Shenango Valley

Pistol shots roared in Farrell as a crowd of picketers—1,500 men, according to the papers—surrounded local hoop and steel wire mills. Paul Prouse, a thirty-five-year-old worker, supposedly fired on a state police trooper, wounding him. A local police officer returned fire and mortally wounded Prouse; the crowd of workers rained bricks and stones on the officer, which started a three-hour street battle that left many injured. Few sought treatment in hospitals, reporters said, for fear that they would be implicated in the fighting.

That day, the Mercer County sheriff swore in three hundred citizen deputies and prepared to march them to the battle site. Officials claimed that eleven people had been shot overnight during the first battle, including a state constable who was shot in the head. "Two foreigners are dead as a result of the rioting," the *Pittsburgh Press* claimed hours after the battle. State police patrolled the streets of New Castle, where scores of newly returned soldiers marched with rifles and patted down anyone who passed through the mill district. "Several of the accused were carrying revolvers and a number of agitators also were taken into custody," reports claimed. In the hardest-hit mill districts, conditions seemed to be approaching those of a civil war.

"Until They Bend the Knee"

The first day was marked by violence, confusion and clashing reports, and the days to come would tell the tale. Strike organizers warned observers to not make snap judgments, as more workers would stream out through the first week. Foster claimed that Jones and Laughlin workers, who had initially demurred, later trickled out of the mill as they saw the strike's effects elsewhere. The Pittsburgh papers made their side of the story clear. The *Press* announced on Tuesday, September 23, "MORE MEN AT WORK—Say Strikers Lose Ground in Local Steel Plants." The *Gazette Times* reported, "SITUATION IMPROVING," and the *Post* said, "STRIKE FAILS TO HALT PITTSBURGH MILLS." Almost everywhere, superintendents eagerly reported that more men were turning out to work, the mill gates were quiet and the plants were running at or near their full capacities. Gertrude Gordon, a *Pittsburgh Press* correspondent covering the first fights, reported more boredom than violence outside the Pittsburgh mills.

It is rather an agreeable surprise, though the lack of thrills, of course, is a little disappointing to a "newspaper person," to go out on what was heralded as the biggest strike ever known and find it as peaceful as a Sunday school picnic. In fact, far more so, for there are plenty of Sunday school picnics which break up into a good old-fashioned row. Yesterday, Pittsburgh was tense with expectation as to what might happen…. "Nothing" was the answer I brought back. Perhaps the rain had something do with the fact that there were no crowds on the street; perhaps it was the sight of the many proclamations calling all to keep the peace which were plastered on every convenient wall in the towns on the outskirts of the city.

Regardless of Ms. Gordon's "lack of thrills" or the superintendents' claims, the strike was having a serious effect on the industry. Stocks remained strong as investors maintained their faith, but pig-iron production in the Pittsburgh district fell by three-eighths in the first week. Police throughout Allegheny County rushed to stop "incipient riots" as striking workers congregated downtown, at the heart of the Pennsylvania steel district. Windows were smashed and police were reportedly attacked in Lawrenceville. Mounted police rushed a large crowd of workers at Penn Avenue and Thirtieth Street

Strike supporters drive a car through the streets. The sign says, "Division 85, Homewood Barn," which refers to a local division of a streetcar operators' union. *Library of Congress.*

and arrested three Polish-born strikers, one of whom allegedly had a pistol. More strikers met at the city's labor halls, despite police threats. The *New York Times* reported that riot insurance rates had tripled throughout the steel district as soon as the strike began. Policies that totaled as much as $200 million were taken out to cover the factories and warehouses around Pittsburgh, the newspaper claimed.

So far, the strike wasn't the total, crushing victory the unions had hoped for, but growing discontent and public meetings showed the unions' power throughout the steel valleys. The national organizing committee claimed that there were 275,000 strikers nationwide on the first day, which ballooned to 350,000 a week later. Even if the industry's lower estimates were true, this was a strike of unprecedented scale in U.S. history. "Employers and workers alike apparently had abandoned their early hopes of a quick, decisive victory," the United Press Wire Service reported on the second day.

> *The steel masters were reported to be bringing stocks of food into their plants and laying plans to defend their mills if necessary, while the strikers were getting ready to carry on industrial warfare for an extended period. Early reports today indicated that although the strikers were losing some ground in the smaller towns of the important Pittsburg district, their strength was greater there than had been admitted by the United States Steel corporation.*

This strike wouldn't be a matter of days or even weeks. While the steel moguls expressed confidence that they could wait out the workers, it was clear that they had exaggerated their power on the first day. Writing after the strike, Foster boasted of the workers' victory in those opening days and declared their action a victory against the bosses' hypocrisy.

> *But in spite of opposition, blundering and treachery, the steel workers had spoken. Mr. Gary was answered. Previous to the strike, he declared that the unions represented an insignificant minority of his men, the great bulk of his working force being satisfied. He compelled the Committee to show its credentials. Result: 365,500 steel workers laid down their tools....The great steel strike thoroughly exposed the hypocrisies of Mr. Gary and his ilk that in some mysterious way labor policies and conditions in the steel industry depend upon the wishes of the body of the workers....No matter how bitter their grievances, when they raise their voice to ask redress, they are discharged, blacklisted, staved, beaten, jailed and even shot, until they bend the knee again and yield to the will of their industrial masters.*

Patience, Faith and Endurance

Father Adalbert Kazincy looked on in horror as state constables drove into a crowd of his parishoners. The forty-eight-year-old Catholic priest, pastor of St. Michael's parish in Braddock where the town's Slovak immigrants worshiped, saw the "iron-hoofed Huns" of the police drive strikers and their families from the church steps on the first day of the strike. Similar violence, some of it deadly, had already struck other steel towns, and Kazincy feared the new attack would drive another outburst. In a letter to Foster just days after the attack, Kazincy wrote, "One could feel that helpless feeling of being lifted up by some invisible force, forced, thrown against the flux of the raging, elemental passion of resentment, against the Kozaks [cossacks] of this State."

Kazincy was among the few clergymen who openly backed the strikers in the Pittsburgh steel district. Some, like the Reverend John Gaynor, offered sermons on "the futility of strikes and exhorting [workers] to remain steadfast to their employers," as the *Daily Post* put it. But with a flock made up of unskilled steelworkers and their young families, Kazincy saw firsthand the rage the men felt toward the "cossacks" and their bosses. Even under regular attacks, he marveled at his parishoners' refusal to draw weapons or provoke further violence. "They moved on, with heads lowered and jaw firmly set, to submit. Oh, it was great; it was magnificent. They, these husky, muscle-bound Titans of raw force walked home...only thinking, thinking hard," he said. "Oh, only for one wink from someone, would there be a puddle of red horseblood mixed with the human kind. But no. We want to win the strike. We want to win the confidence of the public."

Kazincy's church would become a gathering place for the strikers, both Catholic and Protestant, from all the surrounding towns and cities. Threatened by the authorities and running against pressure from his own church leaders, he preached to a packed church on the need to remain steadfast. "I preach to them about their own weapons," he told Vorse, who attended one such sermon. "Against them are violence, lies, repression. They have only their patience, their faith their endurance."

Vorse recalled:

> *The church was packed. Then I saw everyone was going to Father Kazinci's church. There were no labor meetings allowed in McKeesport, no meetings in Rankin; Homestead had one meeting a week. But the steel workers could come hear Father Kazinci preach.*

They made way for me. I managed to squeeze in. In that church, there was an air of happiness. They had escaped the Constabulary. The Constabulary would not follow them to church....The church was more crowded than the organizer's office. Their restlessness and anxiety were gone. They stood quiet, released, free for a moment. Then full-throated this audience sang a chant of the sixth century—men and women and children. The Slovaks have never lost the custom of communal singing.

If the authorities closed his church, Kazincy warned, he would first raise a flag on the steeple to say, "This church was destroyed by the Steel Trust." He was joined by the Reverend Charles Molnar, pastor of Braddock's Slovak Lutheran church and another ally of the strikers. "Before the war and during this war, whenever the government asked something of foreigners, they were willing to do it," Molnar told investigators. "They willingly gave their money buying Liberty Bonds, you know that, their sons and husbands were asked to go to war and they went. But suddenly when this strike came, they are considered dangerous to this country as Bolshevists."

In every town and city where strikers left the mills, they soon formed their own communities and their own means of survival. Despite the mill owners' assurances that the strike was already wavering, repression became more frequent and more heavy-handed. Public meetings were all but impossible

Pittsburgh workers clean and repair a massive ladle used in a steel mill circa 1905. *Library of Congress.*

in most of the towns around Pittsburgh, and many strikers had to walk for miles to city labor halls where they could gather unimpeded. Two Duquesne brothers testified to federal investigators that they were stopped by police and thrown in jail for attending union meetings; when they explained they were headed to the city, the officers said simply, "You won't go to Pittsburgh," and locked them up. Workers in the northern mills around New Castle, Farrell and Sharon crossed into Ohio, where government forces were notably less violent, to attend union meetings. "Here, we are back in America," said one worker to Vorse as they crossed the Ohio line.

John Fitzpatrick, head of the organizing effort, told a Senate committee:

> *Since the strike has been on, the opposition has been unimaginable. The police are there with these mounted horsemen. They will not permit a meeting of any description....In Clairton and Homestead, Duquesne and McKeesport, the authorities there interfere with the legal rights of the men. They won't allow them to meet; they won't allow them to do anything. They just club them and beat them and drive them into the street, and ride into their houses.*

As the days passed, violence continued, and the newspapermen's view of the strike became more muted. Another man died in ongoing battles in Farrell, where hastily deputized civilians clashed with strikers. In Sharon, council members allowed the police chief to nearly double his force, and in New Castle, deputies raided a Polish club and claimed they found rifles and bayonets. Authorities in the area announced plans to deputize dozens of black citizens after realizing that "white Americans were reticent about being sworn in as special deputy sheriffs." The practice of using African Americans as strikebreakers, which was common in areas where they were rebuffed by unions or usually kept from the mills, helped to further divide workers. A woman in Donora told Vorse she was apprehended near a picket line by a "negro" who "pointed a gun at her and arrested her." These accusations were particularly dangerous in late 1919, the year of the so-called Red Summer, during which brutal, racist attacks on black Americans ravaged the country.

Reports of scattered violence flowed in daily. In Natrona, police broke up a meeting of two thousand people. In Otto, near McKeesport, thirty-six were arrested amidst gunfire. In Clairton, officers lying in ambush shot at strikers who had allegedly attacked strikebreakers. Widely circulated newspaper photographs showed helmeted police on horseback clubbing people on the

South Side or "clearing the streets," as the *Pittsburgh Press* put it. Organizers' complaints to Governor William Cameron Sproul fell on deaf ears. "Permit me to take this opportunity," Sproul told Foster, "of saying to you that the situation which now exists, where lawlessness and disorder have compelled the intervention of the state to aid the local authorities to maintain the peace….I shall expect your full cooperation in helping us to see to it that the laws of the commonwealth are observed and its peace preserved." Sproul defended the police and instead accused outside agitators of "(coming) into Pennsylvania to spread wicked propaganda and to endeavor to incite the ignorant and the vicious to riot and pillage."

The strikers were at war with the local authorities, and state officials showed no interest in their demands. They would have to turn their attention to the halls of power in Washington if they were to receive outside help.

The Halls of Power

The scope of the strike, which was raging from the Pittsburgh steel valleys to Chicago and even to Colorado, immediately drew the attention of the U.S. Senate. On the strike's first day, Senator William S. Kenyon of Iowa moved to open a committee investigation into the matter. A day later, it was front-page news in the Pittsburgh papers: Senate investigators would soon be on the ground in Pittsburgh to gather information for public hearings in the days to come.

The union leaders had so far had mixed results from federal involvement. They had benefited from the president's wartime labor committees, but with America now at peace abroad, the pressure to back unions had diminished. After all, President Wilson himself had asked the unions to delay this very strike.

The Senate Education and Labor Committee opened its testimony on September 25, the fourth day of the strike, to hear from Fitzpatrick. The steel union leader detailed the circumstances that led to the battle: the brutal working conditions in the mills, the requests from Pennsylvania workers to organize, the difficulty arranging meetings in steel towns patrolled by private police and state constables. Fitzpatrick expressed hope that a nationwide industrial conference with government, labor and business leaders might break the impasse, but he made plain that the steel bosses' refusal to deal fairly had led to the unions' decision.

Labor leader John Fitzpatrick, *standing*, testifies before a Senate committee for the steel strike. *Library of Congress.*

There is ground now upon which we can get together; but the mere fact of calling a conference would not be sufficient to induce the 350,000 men who have left their employment to return. They have left their employment because of the wrongs done them, because of the brutality that has been practiced against them; because their brothers and sisters have been murdered in cold blood. They resent that, and they will not go back into the mills until they get a more decent consideration; and they are going to ask the United States government to give them just common, ordinary justice, and until that is accorded to them, our opinion is that they will not go back to the mills.

Senators pressed Fitzpatrick on the conditions around Pittsburgh, where meetings were being broken up and gatherings of workers were being trampled by armed police. When asked whether it would benefit the committee to send senators to the steel valleys, Fitzpatrick answered in the affirmative:

It would be a wonderful influence for the committee to go there, to get this idea, and to bring into your presence these men, with their heads beaten

off of them, these women and children that have been trampled on....
This is a crisis in this nation's history, and...unless citizenship in Western
Pennsylvania is immediately given their rights, God knows what is going
to happen.

Further investigation that week centered on AFL chairman Samuel Gompers, who testified to the horrific conditions in the steel mills. But the true test of the committee's purpose would come the following week when Judge Gary, the taciturn, hard-dealing head of the steel trust, was set to testify.

Gary, of course, had long argued that the open shop was the only way forward for the industry. This way, workers were free to unionize individually and deal with the bosses, he said, but there was no need for universal union recognition by U.S. Steel or its smaller competitors. Union allies fought this line. Gary may have taken a laissez-faire approach, they said, but it masked a deeply ingrained opposition to all organized labor. The open shop was merely a cover for the steel bosses' refusal to deal with any union, closed shop or otherwise. Gary's exchange with Montana senator Thomas J. Walsh on October 1, more than a week into the strike, appeared to help their case.

SENATOR WALSH: Was there any other reason for your refusal to hear these [union] *men, to see whether they did represent your men or not, except that your personal investigation satisfied you that they could not enlighten you about the conditions of your workmen and their relationship to your company?*

MR. GARY: Well, I want to be frank enough to say that it has been my policy, and the policy of our corporation, not to deal with union labor leaders.

SENATOR WALSH: Any way, at any time?

MR. GARY: At any time. And for the reason we do not believe in contracting with unions. When an employer contracts with the union labor leaders, he immediately drives all of his employees into the unions.

In Gary's telling, the AFL leaders who had signed his men on by the tens of thousands had done so by trickery and intimidation. He claimed that the leaders had no connection with his workers, and most had chosen to stay at the mills because they saw no benefit in working with outside agitators. The

Judge Elbert Gary, *center foreground*, testifies before the Senate committee investigating the steel strike, 1919. *Library of Congress.*

reality, of course, was far different, but Gary's statement suggested a fair deal with the strikers might be out of the question. The Senate committee would gather hundreds of pages of testimony, but it would get the warring parties no closer to a resolution.

Both sides would get another chance at a grand national industrial conference, which was convened on Wilson's orders during the month of October. On October 6, day fifteen of the strike, fifty-seven leading figures from labor, business and politics gathered in Washington to discuss the future of labor relations in America. The conference wasn't technically planned around the strike, but its attendees knew the urgency of the situation. A front-page article in the *Pittsburgh Daily Post* read:

> *Apparently with the determination of differentiating this conference from many similar gatherings held in Washington, the public's delegates demanded that sessions be held night and day, if necessary, to establish a basis for harmonious relations between capital and labor during the present abnormal economic conditions.*

Those "abnormal economic conditions" still dominated the press, while the steel companies issued fresh claims every day about mills reopening and workers surging back to their posts. Meanwhile, in Gary, Indiana, the steel president's namesake, officials were set to declare martial law and send armed troops of the U.S. Army's Fourth Division to regain control.

Wilson, recovering from a stroke just days earlier, had hoped for a peaceful discussion of the way forward for American labor. But as advisor Bernard Baruch told him, the steel strike "had the effect of focusing interest and attention upon present conflict." Within days of the conference's opening, the labor representatives issued their first resolutions to end the steel strike. They called for a special committee to settle the strike, along with an agreement for workers' return to the mills on the following conditions: the right to organize, collective bargaining agreements, a living wage and a true eight-hour day. The move to put the bosses on the defensive was bold, especially just days after the most powerful man in the steel industry had refused to even recognize unions' existence. Still, some observers felt the resolution was a step in the right direction. "It is the general opinion that prospects for permanent industrial peace is brightening," read an article in the *Daily Post* on October 10. It was an incongruous statement, as it was positioned just inches from a story on raging gun battles with "radicals" in Indiana.

As the days went by and the conference ground on, the steel moguls' resistance only appeared to grow. Near-breakthroughs were scuttled by fights over company unions, the open shop or the terminology used to describe workers' organizations. What appeared to be a brief opening was quickly closed as Gary conferred with his fellow steel bosses during a mid-month break from the proceedings. Some bosses went so far as to suggest he boycott the conference, but in the end, he returned to great public interest. Would Gary come bearing a deal to end the strike, which was then approaching the one-month mark?

The answer, Gary revealed, was "no." There was no grand deal in the works. The steel bosses still refused to deal with unions and resolved to fight the strike to the bitter end. Gary said:

> *I am of the fixed opinion that the pending strike against the steel industry of this country should not be arbitrated or compromised, nor any action taken by the conference which bears upon that subject. Also that there should be maintained in actual practice, without interruption, the open shop as I understand it, namely, that every man, whether he does or does not belong*

Judge Elbert Gary, *second from left*, arrives at a national industrial conference meant to smooth strike tensions and set a postwar labor consensus. *Library of Congress.*

to a labor union, shall have the opportunity to engage in any line of legitimate employment on terms and conditions agreed upon between employee and employer.

Gary did not budge: as long as he was in charge, the unions would never gain full representation in the Pittsburgh mills.

Gary's fellow businessmen applauded the speech, but the union leaders lashed out in response. Gompers warned Gary not to declare victory so soon or so confidently: "Sometimes, swallowing the canary may make indigestible food." Conditions across the country would only deteriorate, he warned, as long as the steel bosses refused to deal fairly with their workers.

The next day, the full conference voted on a series of proposals meant to end the strike or at least reach a preliminary deal. All three bodies of the conference, the unions, the businesses and the government representatives, proposed their own deals for collective bargaining, but none passed. The

President Woodrow Wilson. Wilson sought labor peace, allying with unions during World War I, but stepped back after the conflict. *Library of Congress.*

conference failed to agree on a scheme to resolve the strike, which left its outcome uncertain. The local press took a clear stance on the events; the October 22 *Pittsburgh Daily Post* said, "LABORITES LOSE FIGHT ON STEEL WALKOUT—Industrial Conference Sustains Gary." The newspaper reported, "The president's industrial conference will not attempt to adjudicate the steel strike and it refuses to go on record in favor of collective bargaining as interpreted by the American Federation of Labor." Where the president's handpicked advisors had sided freely with unions throughout the war, their peacetime colleagues no longer felt the need to do so. In a dictated message to those in Washington, an ailing Wilson pleaded with his conference not to fall into hopeless disagreement:

> *At a time when the nations of the world are endeavoring to find a way of avoiding international war, are we to confess that there is no method to be found for carrying on industry except in the spirit and with the very method of war? Must suspicion and hatred and force rule us in civil life? Are our*

industrial leaders and our industrial workers to live together without faith in each other, constantly struggling for advantage over each other, doing naught but what is compelled?

His words had little effect. The conference ended with no significant agreement; an agreement had not even been reached on lesser points and non-binding language. In Pennsylvania, the war went on as before. On the same day the conference shot down proposals to end the strike, a crowd of Braddock union members hurled rocks and bottles at "loyal" Edgar Thomson men until police arrested twenty amidst gunfire.

BOLSHEVIKS, ANARCHISTS AND AGITATORS

All through the steel country, one word was whispered to strike fear into the hearts of police and middle-class newspaper readers: "Bolshevism." The strike was launched just as communism was taking hold in much of Europe, and to businessmen and federal investigators, there was little doubt that the organizers were under the sway of a foreign power. Many of the tactics they used were reminiscent of those underway in civil war–ravaged Germany, including the employment of freshly returned soldiers to disarm and drive off striking workers. Headlines about the strike appeared alongside those of "radical" gun attacks, which were themselves printed alongside updates from Russia, Hungary and Germany. Even in the English-speaking world, Bolshevism seemed to be on the rise; British workers were shutting down industries, and an electoral party that represented their unions was surging in strength.

The first accusations of Bolshevism in Pittsburgh came before the strike even began, as police around western Pennsylvania accused outside agitators of stirring up the "Slavish" immigrant population. These allegations surged within a day of the strike's start, when Foster, the tireless organizer of the steelworkers' committee, was tied to syndicalism and the IWW through his old writings. The *Pittsburgh Press* announced these accusations against Foster one day into the strike:

Accusing William Z. Foster, secretary-treasurer of the national labor committee in charge of organizing the steelworkers of being a Bolshevist sympathizer and the author of I.W.W. writings, Congressman John J. Cooper of Youngstown today, in a speech on the floor of the house, appealed to union labor throughout the United States to reject the counsel of radical agitators whose only purpose is to overthrow the government and destroy constitutional liberty.

Cooper drew out Foster's bright red book, *Syndicalism*, on the House floor, then detailed for his colleagues Foster's sympathy for sabotage, general strike and revolution. "Another passage from Foster's writings," the newspaper announced, "declared the Syndicalist or IWW to be a 'radical anti-patriot, a true internationalist, who knows no country.'"

This was shocking news to conservative-minded union men, who held themselves as patriots looking only for a fair share of the mills' success. Claims of Bolshevism, or of sympathy with the IWW and anarchists, became a key propaganda tool in the fight against the strikers. And while some strikers and leaders certainly kept ties to radical groups, and while the newly formed communist movement clearly sympathized with their cause, the reality was far more complex. Interchurch World Movement investigators, seemingly sympathetic to the strikers but motivated by religious sentiment, tried to silence the claim in a report gathered during the fight:

A stranger in America reading the newspapers during the strike and talking with steel masters both in and out of steel communities must have concluded that the strike represented a serious outbreak of Bolshevism red hot from Russia. The chief memory that American citizens themselves may have a few years from now may well be that the strike was largely the work of Reds. "'Reds' back of the Steel Strike" was a frequent headline in September.

The investigators quoted a *New York Times* article that was printed well into the strike:

Radical leaders planned to develop the recent steel and coal strike into a general strike and ultimately into a revolution to overthrow the government, according to information gathered by federal agents in Friday night's wholesale round-up of members of the Communist parties. These data, officials said, tended to prove that the nation-wide raids had blasted the most menacing revolutionary plot yet unearthed.

Even the mainstream outlets that sought an evenhanded account suggested a direct connection between the ongoing fight and foreign

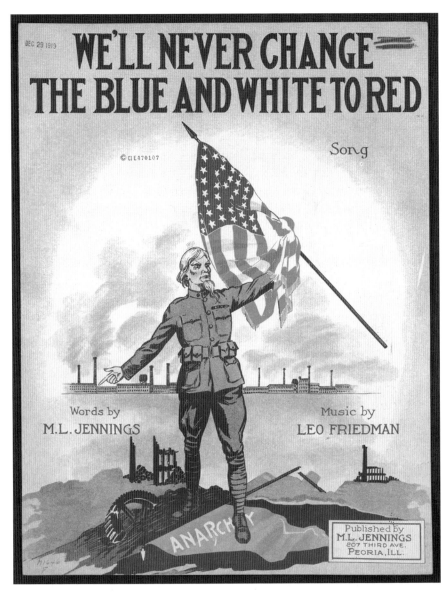

Postwar sheet music demonstrates surging patriotism at the height of the 1919 Red Scare. Uncle Sam steps on the red flag of "anarchy." *Library of Congress.*

radicalism. "Are Steel Strike Leaders Patriots or Bolshevists?" asked a Pittsburgh print advertisement for the *Literary Digest*, which offered evidence for both options. Calls by strike leaders to socialize American industry appeared to tie them to Lenin and Trotsky. An October conference of

Pittsburgh's ethnic Rusyns, a Slavic group hailing from the Carpathian Mountains who settled heavily in Pennsylvania, voted to reject Bolshevism, the IWW and the strike, all at once. A judge presiding over a Philadelphia naturalization ceremony took time to warn the new American citizens that "parlor Bolsheviks" like Foster were the greatest danger before them.

Steel industry leaders were certainly willing to tie the strike to incipient Communism. Gary himself called workers who followed Fitzpatrick and Foster "Bolsheviki" and accused them of seeking "the closed shop, soviets and the forcible distribution of property," as the church investigators recounted. "The organizers were all subversive," a Gary ally said. "They said things to make the labor forces want more than fair wages; made 'em want to share the profits." While many of the union leaders, including Foster, had radical leanings, it was nigh impossible to demonstrate that the workers had been radicalized by Foster's blood-red book on syndicalism. The book had been out of print for years, and police never reported finding copies in strikers' possession.

Claims of Bolshevism and syndicalism drew the eye of the federal government, which was already sweeping cities for communist sympathizers. During their lengthy committee investigation into the strike, senators took time to probe Foster on his radical views and his now-famous book. "Are you a believer in syndicalism in any form?" asked one senator of Foster, pressing him to either recant his past writings or accept that he still believed them. Foster maintained that he was a syndicalist, but under a different definition— he merely held to the ideals of labor unionism now, not to the ideas he had written about years prior. Other labor leaders held themselves as the only alternative to foreign radicalism, the only shield American bosses had to stop its attack. By crushing the steelworkers' demands for fair treatment and shorter hours, the labor bosses had opened the door to Russian-style extremists, organizers claimed. Gompers himself presented the senators with a lengthy article on the dangers of Bolshevism, of forced labor, autocracy and supposed German influence.

Of course, with the strike drawing national attention and workers dying in gun battles and police attacks, America's radicals soon took note. On the eve of the walkout, the *New York Call*, a socialist newspaper, praised the workers and the fight to come. The New York socialists foresaw the worst of the allegations even before they were revealed:

> *Unless all signs fail, this steel strike will be long and costly. Steel is fundamental to all manufacturing industry, and there will be endless millions*

of dollars at the disposal of the steel trust, coming from the other employers that are standing out against democracy in the shops. Not only will the bosses employ every sort of intimidation, from blackjacks to machine guns, but they will try all kinds of trickery to stampede the men back into the plants. One trick is in evidence already—a campaign to discredit William Z. Foster, who has been in general charge of the field organizer in the steel mills for the past year. Foster organized the workers in the stockyards and meat packing plants two years ago. The packers hate him. The game is to represent him as a dangerous anarchist.

The American communist movement, which was merely weeks old as the strike unfolded, quickly latched on to the struggle. The second-ever issue of *The Communist*, the newspaper of the immigrant-dominated Communist Party of America, featured the steel strike in a wall of text on its front page. "The final answer to all these garbled statements of 'improvements' is the workers' revolt itself," the article proclaimed. "The workers are determined to conquer real improvements; and as they struggle for this lesser objective, they will develop the consciousness of the larger objective—the conquest of capitalism." The communist newspaper decried the forming of anti-union militias and deputy forces in the Monongahela Valley, comparing them to the "bourgeois white guards" who repressed organized labor from Finland to Hungary.

These magazines, newspapers and pamphlets inevitably made their way to the workers in Pittsburgh, especially those who had been most active in organizing the mills. One observer said millworkers often ignored the Pittsburgh newspapers but eagerly circulated faded and stained copies of *The Call*, *Appeal to Reason*, *The Toiler* and other radical publications. Rank-and-file leaders, the Interchurch World Movement found, "had no labor reputations to preserve against charges of Bolshevism. They used as assistants the boldest and most energetic spirits and these were frequently readers of the only sort of labor papers customarily circulating among unorganized workers, that is, socialist and I.W.W. papers. The organizers looked to their followers, men speaking thirty different dialects, and did not mind if some of the followers imbibed ambitious ideas about 'ending the rule of the bosses.' But it took very few repetitions of these ambitions, in broken English, to the mill bosses to spread the fear that the 'foreigners' had revolutionary intentions."

Organizers strained to preserve their reputations when foreign-language leaflets edged too close to radicalism. One English leaflet ended poetically with the phrase: "Forward to bleed and die!" which, when translated into

Polish, becomes, "Forward to wade through blood!" That distinction frightened a Polish organizer, who supposedly argued, "My people are all good Catholics. They won't stand for advice like that." Religious leaders tried to tamp down radical ideas and insisted their followers weren't under the sway of foreign powers. When Molnar, the Slovak Lutheran pastor of Braddock, defended his striking congregants, he stressed that they had nothing to do with Bolshevism. "No, gentlemen, we are not Bolshevists; we are not anarchists; we are not socialists—we are Christians and we are trying to do the best for the government we can," he said. "We love this country, and as for myself, I am trying to be the best citizen I can and so I am leading my people. It is absolutely unfair to accuse these people, especially the Slovaks, even if they are strikers now."

6

FAILURE WAS WRITTEN

As the Senate finished its early testimony and Wilson gathered his doomed labor peace conference, the war in the steel district continued apace. Officials in West Virginia learned on September 26 that an army of thousands of steelworkers planned to cross the Ohio River from Steubenville, Ohio, if plants in Weirton, West Virginia, failed to close. The head of the Steubenville strike committee offered a warning that could be interpreted as a veiled threat: "I can't stop them; neither can anyone else. They are determined to go there." The governor of West Virginia sent an urgent telegram to his counterpart in Ohio, warning him that a body of five thousand men might be gathering to cross into West Virginia. If that were to happen, he said, "any such effort will be regarded as an attack upon the sovereignty of West Virginia."

The assault never materialized and Weirton workers walked off peacefully, but lurid reports of armed battalions and gun battles dominated the news in Pittsburgh. Months earlier, during the run-up to the strike, officials claimed that Russian anarchist miners were organizing a march on the Monongahela Valley, and now another rural army seemed hellbent on marching up the steel valleys. All of this news came as workers in eastern Pennsylvania's Bethlehem Steel plants prepared to join the strike after several days' delay. In Ohio, where conditions were marginally better, organizers plotted to aid their Pennsylvania comrades. "We are going to flood Pennsylvania with organizers and see if we can't annex it to the United States," said one organizer to the *Pittsburgh Daily Post*. Other leaders boasted of a "young army" of picketers that was closing mills in the Shenango Valley.

State police in Farrell told stories of a high-powered rifle, supposedly "of Russian make," that was passed between striking workers and used in an effort to detonate a tank of explosive chemicals. Police said they had already killed one gunman, who was identified only as "a Serbian," but were on the hunt for more snipers. The stories told in the newspapers appeared fantastic at times, especially when they appeared between daily updates on the strike's never-ending demise.

By early October, the strike had settled into a familiar rhythm; newspapers described each "round" as though a boxing match was underway. The nation's attention turned to the World Series and to Wilson's ill health, but every day, the steel bosses reported more workers returning to work. The Senate investigation was still underway, and the national industrial conference was just being seated when the mill owners felt confident enough to issue full-page advertisements in the Pittsburgh papers. In these advertisements, Uncle Sam announced in eight languages, "The Strike Has Failed—GO BACK TO WORK," and a smoke-churning steel mill stood behind him. Calling out to workers from Poland, Italy, Russia and the Balkan nations, the ad offered no doubt that the strikers' cause was lost:

> The end of the steel strike is in sight. Failure was written across it before it was a day old.
> American workers who understood the radical element that is seeking to operate under the cloak of organized labor are now back. Few of them ever left their work—only a few foreign-born—mostly aliens, who allowed themselves to be swayed by the un-American teachings of radical strike agitators. Sane heads in labor's own ranks have saved American liberty in this great struggle and have again demonstrated that nothing short of one hundred percent Americanism can hope to win out in this country.
> The strike has failed. GO BACK TO WORK.

The foreign-language segments were blunter in their accusations: "The steel industry strike…is led by men who are trying to establish the red government of anarchy and Bolshevism in this land of opportunity and freedom," one section read.

Every day, the crackdowns grew more severe. In Gary, Indiana, the army claimed full control after days of violence. Photographs showed uniformed soldiers in campaign hats, standing guard behind a water-cooled machine gun in a truck bed as they enforced a declaration of martial law. A two-man "riot squad" rode in a motorcycle and sidecar to control the public

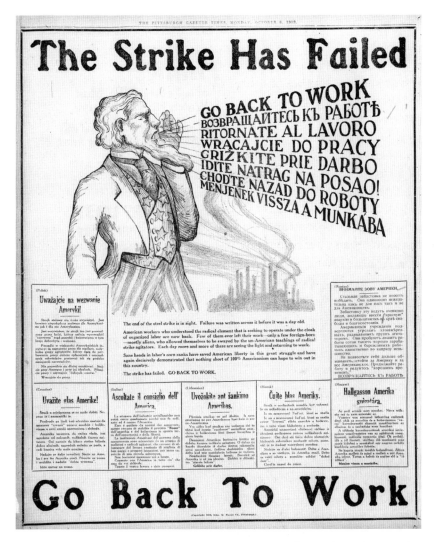

A full-page advertisement in the October 6, 1919 *Pittsburgh Gazette Times* calls on workers to return to the mills in eight languages. Pittsburgh Gazette Times *via Newspapers.com.*

right-of-way. In Weirton, police supposedly arrested more than one hundred IWW members, many of them of Finnish descent, and marched them to the city center, where they were forced to kiss the American flag before a cheering crowd. The newspapermen could hardly contain their excitement. "Finn Red Guards Quake in Fear as Stalwart Ex-Marine Commands Them Kneel," the *Pittsburgh Press* said, pointing out that many of the humiliated Wobblies hailed from Woodlawn, near Aliquippa. Word spread of a vicious gun battle between "steel strikers and negroes" in Donora, where at least one immigrant striker was reportedly left seriously wounded.

In the immigrant shantytowns of the Ohio Valley, the elderly Irish-born organizer Mother Jones moved from village to village, keeping the strikers' hopes up and urging them to defend their families. To those who feared being labeled Bolsheviks, Jones had a simple reply: "Afraid? There's only one thing you should be afraid of—of not being a man!" Vorse, the British journalist, moved through the valleys too. She spoke with Allegheny County workers who dreaded the label of "scab" and Weirton men who said the mere appearance of socialist literature would bring the police crashing in.

In Steubenville, Vorse spoke with Serbian immigrants who had fought for their country in World War I and who now carried on the fight as strikers:

> *I stood waiting to cross the noisy street. Trucks slam-banged past. The engine on the railway overhead hooted. A man beside me was whistling. He was whistling Tamo Dalecko, the song which the Serbians sang in exile. After the great defeat in 1915 by the Austrians they retreated over the Ibar Pass, went over the Albanian hills. They went to Corfu. They reconstructed their regiments and when everyone thought Serbia dead, Serbian regiments appeared on the Bulgarian front. Tamo Dalecko was the song for a defeated nation. But the Serbs sang it when they marched to victory.*
>
> *"Where did you learn that song?" I asked him.*
>
> *"In Corfu. My father was a Serb in the banat. When war come, I go home. I march on the great retreat."*
>
> *"How did you get back here?" I asked him.*
>
> *"I get wounded on Monastir front. I am American citizen. They send me home from France."*
>
> *"Are you striking?" I asked him.*
>
> *The jam of the street loosened up. He strode on ahead. He threw at me over his shoulder, "Sure I strike."*
>
> *From his abundant gayety he turned to wave at me and went off singing to win the strike. His smile had the assurance of victory. He made me understand the strike. The brothers of these men working in the steel mills had overthrown Czar and Austrian Kaiser. In America they fought Gary.*

Spies and Informants

Agent Z-16 listened closely as three Russian men talked outside the Monessen post office. Looking unremarkable in dark suits and caps, the men were discussing a bomb that had exploded in the town two days earlier.

"I am pretty sure I know who did it," one said.

"I have pretty good dope on it myself," another replied.

The men separated briefly, then met again—Z-16 watching all the time. When they stepped aboard a streetcar and crossed the Monongahela toward the city, he followed. When they got off at the corner of Smithfield Street and Carson Street on the South Side, he did the same. The group walked a few blocks, then disappeared. Only when he could no longer track them by himself did Z-16 stop two police officers and ask for their help. "One of the officers asked me if I had a badge," Z-16 recalled, "to which I replied in the negative."

The man identified in investigators' reports as Z-16 wasn't a police officer, a federal agent or a deputy; he was a private industrial spy—one of hundreds employed by mill owners in Pittsburgh before and during the steel strike. Operating under a collection of private agencies—some shady, some advertised openly—they infiltrated unions, disrupted meetings, stirred up dissent and reported every detail to their bosses. The labor spies claimed to provide industrial peace, but they operated as a paramilitary force, organized into squads with their identities kept secret even from their fellow spies.

"In one way or another they are hired, 'trained' and planted in the field, where they remain unknown to each other and often to the company for whose benefit the reports are made," found an extensive investigation by the Interchurch World Movement. The spies, many of whom were of the same ethnic backgrounds as the steelworkers and strikers, got jobs in the mills and worked their way into the union movement. The same report went on to say, "Once located among the foreign element, dressed like them, speaking their language, the next steps to gaining their confidence, their ears and their secrets are rapidly made." Those with no union background came up with excuses for their sudden appearance—one claimed that he had fallen behind on dues so was off the books—and soon launched into conversation with their countrymen.

Experienced union men recognized the marks of an infiltrator, and newcomers with a sudden interest in the strike could face detailed questioning. Strike leaders soon realized there were spies among them, and they made sure to inform their comrades publicly, as another agent, "X-199," said:

[A speaker] *addressing the audience…in his native tongue…states that he was making use of his native tongue so that the detectives present at the meeting would not understand what he was saying. In a meeting when one of the organizers asked those men who were for remaining on strike to raise their hands, and as naturally no one could disobey and they all raised their hands…then Feeney said he knew that there were numerous detectives in the crowd, putting down every word he said, and so he did not expect all the men to stay out that had raised their hands.*

The game of cat and mouse took its toll on the strikers, who knew spies were listening for radical talk they could pass along to the authorities. Labor spies looked for Bolshevik sympathizers and extremists among the ranks. "At a meeting yesterday, a Slav was talking, and he was telling the people how fine the Bolsheviki were," one spy report stated. Another claimed that strikers were attacking "capitalism, of which Gary was the head."

Beyond gathering information, the spies were tasked with breaking the strikers' morale and pushing men back to work. "Their duties are, first, to find out how the strike is going, who the leaders are and what they are saying; second, to destroy the effect of the strike meetings and leaders by counter-propaganda," the church report stated. "In other words, they are detectives and strike breakers both in one." Meeting with the men privately or in small groups, the spies would question how long the strikers' money and supplies would last, which would cast a dark pall on the workers' attitudes. Sympathy strikes appeared possible? They would never happen, X-199 answered. You have enough cash to get by a little longer? It won't last through the strike, Z-16 explained. Though he may have been exaggerating, Z-16 claimed to have personally returned one hundred strikers to work.

The spies worked for businesses like the Corporation Auxiliary Co. or the Sherman Service Co., which kept vast networks in many industrial cities. The agents themselves sometimes lied and exaggerated their findings to get more work, particularly when it involved "reds." Despite the exaggerations, the companies clearly had a successful record. Headquartered locally in a nondescript office of the Wabash Building on what would now be the corner of Liberty Avenue and Stanwix Street, the Corporation Auxiliary agency operated from New York to St. Louis. The steel companies had their own spies, but when they proved insufficient, many turned to the Corporation Auxiliary and its roster of five hundred steel mill agents.

Officials circulated propaganda and training manuals among their men; much of it was reminiscent of religious literature.

> *One way is to help you by suggestions, ideas, lines of argument and so on, to spread the gospel of good cheer, harmony, contentment, confidence and satisfaction among the men with whom you work. In other words, assist you to become propagandists of progress and well-being for the sake of the company, the men and yourself.... Why is it that the things which are done for the workmen's benefit are looked on with suspicion by the men? The company needs your work and realizes that it must have your confidence if you are to be a good workman, and it does its best to treat its men right and do what it can for them. Why not have confidence in this and give the concern a chance to make good the same as the concern is giving you a chance?*

Through these methods, the companies sought not only to spy on labor but to control it entirely. The head of the Corporation Auxiliary Co. told investigators he already had men working as ranking union officers and expected to one day infiltrate organized labor at the highest levels. He said, "We might expect in that way to have men as international officers or even members of the State Federation of Labor." Just as the Federal Bureau of Investigation had an undercover agent among the founding members of the Pittsburgh IWW, so did private businesses hope to control the unions from the ground up. In many places, these goals overlapped. "It is undeniable that labor policies in the steel industry rest in considerable part on the reports of 'under-cover men' paid directly by the steel companies or hired from concerns popularly known as 'strike busters,'" the church investigators wrote. "The 'operatives' make money by detecting 'unionism' one day and 'Bolshevism' the next."

Where controlling the unions failed, spies also sought to divide the steel strikers. In Gary, Indiana, the Sherman Service Co., which billed itself as an "industrial efficiency" company, was accused of intentionally stirring hatred between Italian and Serbian workers to crush the steel strike there. In a letter reprinted by investigators and dated October 2, barely a week into the strike, a Sherman service official called on his agents to provoke "racial hatred" between the groups, whose home countries were embroiled in a military dispute at the time.

> *We want you to stir as much bad feeling as you possibly can between the Serbians and Italians. Spread data among the Serbians that the Italians are going back to work. Call up every question you can in reference to racial*

Armed state constables patrol the streets on horseback in McKees Rocks circa 1909. Residents fought officers in open gun battles. *Library of Congress.*

hatred between these two nationalities: Make them realize to the fullest extent that far better results would be accomplished if they will go back to work. Urge them to go back to work or the Italians will get their jobs.

Operating from the Chicago steel district to the Pittsburgh valleys, these companies were handsomely rewarded. As an investigation in the *New Republic* noted in 1920, the Sherman Service Co. was wealthy enough to defend itself in full-page advertisements in the *New York Times.* Reporters claimed that agents were exempt from the military draft and operated in seemingly every business in the country, from massive textile mills to Thomas Edison's laboratory.

"The scale of organization of industrial espionage stifles any doubt of its scope. Only a tremendous clientele can justify it," said the writer, Sidney Howard, in his investigation. "It operates through the secret service departments of great corporations; the railroads, the United States Steel corporation....It would be interesting to know how many men the business employs. One can only guess at thousands."

The great steel strike ground on, first by weeks, then by months, and the spies' tactics only became more effective. No great victory was on the horizon, and many workers felt that any type of victory was slipping from their grasp.

"THE OPENING HAD BEEN MADE"

Father Kazincy looked out over Braddock from his living room window. From this vantage point, the Slovak priest could see his parish church, the Edgar Thomson Steel Works and the Monongahela below. To Vorse, his interlocutor, he wondered aloud how his striking parishoners could muster the fortitude to keep fighting as the weeks passed.

"Think what sacrifice every day means, what desperate resistance. These people have given up their income voluntarily," Kazincy said. "They have risked their jobs, their only source of income." The immigrants did not spend their money the way American-born workers did; they saved every possible penny in the hope that they could one day secure better lives for their families. However, weeks without work and no end in sight forced them to spend their savings to survive. When a plant superintendent asked a worker on the street whether or not he was returning, the worker answered defiantly, "I'm on strike; I'm taking a holiday. I'm paying myself back those twenty Christmases I worked for the company."

But the struggle couldn't last forever. Families were growing hungry, and the unions' strike fund would never cover the needs of hundreds of thousands of men and their wives and children. "Ordinarily in strikes, the main body of men are able to take care of themselves over an extended period," Foster said. "The danger point is in the poverty-stricken minority. From them come the hunger-driven scabs who so demoralize and discourage the men still out." As the largest strike in American history, the steel battle presented a special challenge for organizers, who in the past had relied on regular union dues to pay funds to men on the picket line. But with much of the industry on strike and very little money trickling in, they decided to serve the workers directly; they opened commissaries to feed the steel towns themselves.

Based in Pittsburgh, the unprecedented nationwide effort drew unions and cooperative organizations together. Organizers in forty-five districts got checks from the national organizing committee, which they then spent locally on tremendous quantities of food. "It finally developed into a huge affair. Few strikers had to be turned away for lack of food," Foster said. The unions ran the operation like a small government. Rations were distributed two days each week and set by family size, with prominent signs telling each family just how much they would get. A family of five or fewer might get eight pounds of beans, eight loaves of bread and four

Hill District tenements circa 1914. The Hill District, home to a large Jewish population, was the site of an IWW-organized stogie makers' strike. *Pittsburgh city photographer via Historic Pittsburgh.*

cans of vegetables each week, plus servings of meat, sauerkraut, milk and coffee. This alone was not enough to sustain parents and children, but it was enough to relieve their struggle.

Vorse had this to say when she visited the Braddock commissary:

> *Any child in the street could tell you where the commissary was....Men passed, big parcels of food in their arms. Two children were tugging their basket up a [set of] narrow basement stairs. Groups of people were standing around. The basement was crowded. In the middle stood counters made of boards and trestles. All around barrels of potatoes, pyramids of canned goods. The smell of coffee was in the air; piles of good bread ready to be given out....It was a long line; Central Europe packed together, Pole, Slovak, Croat, Romanian, Italian. All could have gone back to work had they chosen; there was no picket line in Braddock to shame them. There was everything to drive them back.*

When families applied for benefits, union representatives stopped by their homes to assess their needs. Some families proudly refused to accept aid until the situation was truly dire, sometimes even after that. A Polish family, who was sleeping in a Pittsburgh cellar without any food, decided they could wait another three weeks, Vorse reported. "They had nothing and they could wait three weeks more. The endurance of women was a bulwark of the steel strike. Women like this, young and burdened down by the cares of their children, upheld it."

Autumn drove harder and the steel district got colder, still with no resolution. In those cities where the workers stubbornly refused to return, the mill bosses and local authorities took it upon themselves to force the matter. Some used replacement workers, others simply set angry crowds or armed forces after them.

Such was the case in Johnstown, where the Cambria Steel Co. was operated. Workers there had walked off almost universally in September 1919. In November, they remained steadfast, even after the Federal Labor Commission had failed and the president's pleas had gone unheeded. Foster was scheduled to speak there on November 7, but when he arrived at the train station, locals warned him to turn back. First newspaper reporters, then city police both cautioned Foster not to make his speech. "I demanded protection, but it was not forthcoming," he wrote. "I was told to leave." As he walked through the street toward the city's labor hall, a mob of dozens rushed his entourage. "[T]hey stuck guns against my ribs and took me to the depot. While there, they made a cowardly attempt to force me to sign a back-to-work card, which meant to write myself down a scab." Foster was sent on a train to Conemaugh, outside of the city, flanked by members of the pro-business Citizens Committee that had carried out the attack.

Later that night, Vorse wrote, the committee surrounded the union hall and forced the organizers to leave. "There was no police protection for Foster. The state constabulary were quiet," she wrote. "When mobs are made up of leading citizens, mobs are unmolested." The organizers returned in the weeks to come, and efforts to silence them, first by the Citizens Committee, then by state constables, failed. Offers by union leaders to provide their own armed security in the city were rebuffed. By late November, the struggle had taken its toll, and the first handful of workers returned to the Cambria mills. It was a small number, but the psychological effect was severe. "It was advertised through the papers," Vorse said. "Of the eighteen thousand men on strike only eight hundred went back. But the opening had been made.

Smoke rolled up the sky. In these mills where no smoke had been, the fire of the blast took the heart from the men."

On the strike's nine-week mark, November 24, the *Pittsburgh Daily Post* issued a front-page tally of its cost so far. More than one hundred thousand men had returned to work, they claimed, but tens of thousands more had left the industry entirely, creating a fresh labor shortage. An estimated $30 million worth of labor time had been lost, and the number grew larger every day. More than ten thousand immigrant workers had returned to their homelands since September 22, and fifteen thousand strikers and political radicals had "either left this district or were forced to leave." The mill owners had slowly adjusted to the shortage and either imported new workers or hired from populations that were once considered unacceptable. "Many negroes, Greeks and Mexicans have been brought into this district since the strike began," the *Pittsburgh Daily Post* reported. "Significant are reports showing that the strike has stimulated inventiveness in the management of steel plants....These labor-saving methods will continue to be used." Strikers' hope for victory turned to bitterness and anger against those working in their stead, especially the "negroes" who were now running some of the mills.

Foster recalled that some employers who were fed up with waiting for men to return to work, including those in Butler, Natrona and the Monongahela Valley, evicted families from their company-owned homes or foreclosed on mortgages. He wrote, "Threats of such action drove thousands back to work, it being peculiarly terrifying to workers to find themselves deprived of their homes in winter time. Where evictions actually occurred the victims usually had to leave town or find crowded quarters with other strikers."

Winter was approaching, and there was little reason for the workers to hope. As waves of strikers streamed back to the mills, defeated, the only good news came from elsewhere in the country, where other cities and other industries were convulsed with strikes of their own. The strikers got a gasp of air—however brief—when the miners of western Pennsylvania launched their own battle.

7

THE FINAL STRUGGLE

The headline of the November 1, 1919 *Pittsburgh Press* was enough to strike fear into the heart of any business owner in the mountainous region of western Pennsylvania and West Virginia: "FOUR HUNDRED THOUSAND MINERS ANSWER STRIKE CALL."

Days after the Federal Commission had failed to resolve the steel strike, the nation's coal miners, whose work heated homes, powered trains and kept the mills running, launched a historic strike under the United Mine Workers of America (UMWA). Tens of thousands worked in the district that covered western Pennsylvania.

The battle was a long time coming, and it shared its origins with the steel strike. Back then, coal country stretched from its old outposts in northeastern Pennsylvania to Cambria and Somerset Counties, and from there, it expanded across the southwest, which encompassed the steel trust's "captive mines" in the Allegheny and Kiski Valleys, the Connellsville coke fields and the West Virginia valleys. The men who worked in the mines hailed from rural America, Italy, Russia and every new nation of eastern Europe. They had enjoyed steady work through the war, when their product was considered a military asset and their labor got the attendant government support. As in the steel mills, union efforts were tolerated and even backed at the federal level, so long as the workers remained at their jobs and production didn't halt. However, the war's end left the men without that support.

A wartime agreement with the UMWA forbade strikes, and federal officials hoped to extend that arrangement for as long as possible. Despite growing complaints over inflation, stagnant wages and skyrocketing shareholder profits, union bosses had to tamp down their members' anger in the face of illegal wildcat strikes, but the center couldn't hold for long. At a mass meeting in the Illinois mine district, rank-and-file workers demanded that "all industries be turned over to the working class." Members denounced their union leaders, formed bottom-up organizing committees and called for independent strikes—a call some locals followed.

In Coral, Indiana County, workers at a non-union mine struck in April demanding recognition. They were quickly labeled "Bolsheviks," and local newspapers insisted that miners had no reason to complain, as their wages were above the union rate. The only possible explanation for the unrest, they argued, was radical interference. The *Indiana Evening Gazette* said, "Ninety-five percent of the workmen are ready to return to work… provided they are protected against the Bolsheviks, who are terrorizing the industrial sections of the Indiana valley." Hundreds of locals formed the American Defense Society of Indiana County, a group deputized by the sheriff to stop "anarchy, which already [had] gained a foothold in Indiana County." A post office inspector reported the Coral postmaster as a Bolshevik sympathizer, threatening the man's job. The rural red scare nearly crippled the miners there, but their year-long strike would ultimately win union recognition. To the west, in the "Black Valley" where coal fed the steel mills, the local strike ended with Fannie Sellins's gruesome death at the hands of sheriff's deputies.

In summer 1919, with the steelworkers organizing by the tens of thousands and battles raging in the western Pennsylvania valleys, the most militant coal miners across the country saw their chance to act. They called for a strike vote at the union's August convention in Cleveland and secured an agreement to walk off in November if a new contract wasn't reached. Members endorsed a 60 percent pay hike, shorter and more evenly distributed hours, as well as radical programs like the Plumb Plan, under which the federal government would nationalize the railroads and turn over half their profits to the workers. "When hostilities ceased last November, the miners found themselves in the paradoxical position where their intensive labor was being used to further enrich the owners of coal mines and merchants dealing in coal," said union leaders in a joint statement. "Of course, the mine owners readily conceived that an over-abundance of mined coal would seriously disturb the high prices of coal and endanger their large margin of profits." To the bosses, this talk was straight from the Bolshevik playbook. One representative of

Striking Pennsylvania coal miners show off deputies' rifles at their camp in the early twentieth century. *Library of Congress.*

the mine owners claimed Lenin and Trotsky themselves had ordered the strike. Attorney General Palmer said the strike "challenges the supremacy of the law."

Federal officials warned that they would consider the walkout illegal, but the miners weren't deterred. On the afternoon of October 31, hundreds of thousands—including a reported forty-two thousand in the Pittsburgh district—left the mines with their tools, with no intention of returning. The handful of night-shift miners walked off at midnight. The mine owners had hoped that the threat of a federal injunction would urge the men back to work, but, as the *Pittsburgh Daily Post* reported, "They admitted last evening that it looked as if the injunction would be ignored by the miners." Around Pittsburgh, bosses acknowledged that the strike was 95 percent successful. It was an emergency: Without coal, major industries would shut down and cities would go cold during the winter. Officials seized train cars loaded with coal and diverted them to industries they deemed "essential to the welfare of the nation." Power plant operators insisted they had as much as two months' worth of fuel in reserve, but some suggested the true supply would last no more than three weeks. Pittsburgh officials sought the right to oversee fuel distribution locally, in case supply lines ran low. The government was taking no chances. Troops were readied to guard non-union plants where thousands remained on the job.

The real threat lay in the possibility of the unions joining together. Leaders of the Brotherhood of Railroad Trainmen, which represented rail workers, said they would "assist the miners in every honorable and consistent way." At a meeting of labor leaders, many of them involved in the ongoing steel strike, Vorse reported a growing feeling of solidarity. "The sense of that meeting was that coal, steel and iron belonged together, and that they should use their power together," she wrote.

The coal fight dragged on for a week before a federal judge issued an injunction that ordered the men back to work. UMWA leaders had four days to return their men to the pits. Pittsburgh reporters seemed upbeat about a resolution; a union official told the *United Press Service*, "We are going to use everything in our power to induce the men to return to work." Even if the men didn't return, federal investigators already had plans in the works to round up the most prominent "Bolsheviks" among them—by force if necessary.

"EVERY MAN A RED-HOT ANARCHIST"

It was well after sunset, 8:45 p.m., on November 7, 1919, when police and federal agents crashed into the so-called People's House on New York's East Fifteenth Street. Officers rifled through the Russian anarchist office's papers, seized their books and marched its visitors to the building's fourteenth floor for interrogation. A reporter for New York's socialist paper, the *New York Call*, described the scene dramatically:

> *Clubs and, according to some of the victims, blackjacks were used without mercy. Nearly one hundred prisoners, including eight women, were rushed down to the Department of Justice office, in the Park Row building, in police patrols....A witness of the event said that he saw one of the Russians trying to rush out of the building, his face and clothing covered in blood. Agonized cries were heard.*

A federal official told reporters that the New York raid was only one of many taking place that night, the second anniversary of Russia's October

Revolution. The government was cracking down on "anarchists and revolutionists" who hoped to launch a rebellion of their own in America, he said. Reports began to trickle out in the coming days: police in the East Hills town of Universal, Allegheny County, had arrested two Russian "active agitators," Mike Gedtero and Mike Deglertino. They had picked up at least two more in Monessen, including the alleged "red" Frank Ezeriski.

Most of those rounded up were accused of being members of the Union of Russian Workers (or Union of Russian Workingmen), a little-known group that had operated in the United States for more than a decade. With chapters across the country, the union served mostly as a gathering place for lonely Russian immigrants, many of whom couldn't read or speak English. The group identified with the Russian anarchist tradition that had influenced men like Frick's attacker, Alexander Berkman, and churned out pamphlets and books explaining their revolutionary goals. The titles alone—*Stateless Communism and Syndicalism* and *Manifesto of the Communist-Anarchists*—were enough to frighten federal investigators. Months before the raids, a federal undercover agent wrote a brief history of the group for his superiors, complete with a glossary to explain the definitions of "communism" and "anarchy."

Alexander Berkman, would-be assassin of Henry Clay Frick, addresses a crowd of anarchists in New York in 1914. *Library of Congress.*

In Pittsburgh, as the historian Charles H. McCormick notes, the local Union of Russian Workers posed little threat. While agents had reported hundreds of members in the city, Duquesne, McKees Rocks and Homestead during the war, in 1919, only a handful gathered for Sunday picnics in city parks. Pittsburgh may have been the "center for Russian anarchists in this country," but investigators seemed to find few ties between the Union of Russian Workers and other radical groups like the IWW.

It was just outside the city, in the hills and mountains where the coal strike raged, where the union represented the greatest danger. Thousands of Russians worked in the mines, many isolated in their own communities in the Pennsylvania and West Virginia hills.

The timing was perfect for an assault on the Russian radicals in the coal industry. By cracking down on the most prominent labor activists amongst the Russians, federal agents acknowledged that they could help bring the miners' strike to a speedier end. "[If] these men were removed from their special localities and their un-American agitation stopped it would have a wholesome and immediate effect in the local strike efforts," wrote one federal agent. A federal law passed in 1918 empowered the government to immediately deport foreign radicals of all stripes, even if they hadn't committed a crime. Membership in a group like the Union of Russian Workers was enough to be sent home. Fear of Russian meddling was at its height; the November 5, 1919 *Pittsburgh Gazette Times* announced, "RUSSIAN REDS AIM BLOW AT RULE OF U.S." This issue also detailed Bolshevik efforts, which were funded with gold looted from the Tsar, to overthrow the U.S. government with "propaganda of violence and unreason."

In the West Virginia mining country around Morgantown, the press was alight with reports of Russian treachery. The vast majority of miners had ignored their union's call to comply with a court order and return to work, and the police knew who to blame. The Fairmont *West Virginian* called the Pennsylvania border county of Monongalia "the worst hot bed of radicalism in West Virginia." One issue detailed a strike meeting of immigrant miners:

> *Many Russians, it was said, were in the audience and so many cries of "no end" came from the audience that leaders of the movement to have the men go back to work decided not to put the question to a vote....Radicals have been hard at work among the men, using every possible argument to keep them from returning to work.*

The local sheriff claimed to have discovered a new IWW local along the Monongahela River, miles from the Pennsylvania line.

Days later, federal agents launched a new assault in the coal country. Officers burst into rural "People's Houses" that belonged to the Union of Russian Workers, surprising immigrant miners who in some cases didn't understand why they were under arrest. They found signs of radicalism—photographs of Lenin and Trotsky, red and black crepe paper, a handful of Russian books and pamphlets—but few weapons were found, and there was little to suggest that these poor miners planned to overthrow the government. Nevertheless, dozens were rounded up, to the glee of the local press. On November 17, the *West Virginian* boasted that twenty-nine had been taken to the county jail, "every man a red-hot anarchist."

> *Starting last week, E. W. Lambeth, very special agent from the department of justice, working under Colonel Walker, federal district attorney, together with an almost unbelievable number of plain-clothes scouts have been combing Marion County so thoroughly that scarcely a Red dares to say his own name in the dark. At Morgantown twelve men up to date are in jail, arrested as Bolshevik persons....Sixty thousand Bolshevik are being overshadowed at this time who have been secretly and religiously at work all over the country plotting the overthrow of the United States government.*

More arrests were soon to come. The jails in northern West Virginia swelled with Russians, and county courthouses processed them in bunches with the aid of interpreters. "These men will be taken immediately to Pittsburgh under heavy guard, where they may lie in jail all winter until a port to Russia is open for them," the Fairmont *West Virginian* reported.

THE SOVIET ARK

"Get ready at once," said the prison guards at Ellis Island to Alexander Berkman and his comrades.

At fifty-nine years old, Berkman was no longer the angry young anarchist who had nearly assassinated Henry Clay Frick twenty-seven years earlier. After his release from prison, Berkman had carried on his political work alongside Emma Goldman and an ever-changing circle of left-wing writers and activists, many of whom were born in the Russian Empire. Berkman and Goldman were arrested again in 1917 for interfering with the war effort, but the war was over, and they were now imprisoned as alien radicals, Bolshevik sympathizers—no different from the Pennsylvania millworkers and West Virginia miners who shared their jail at Ellis Island.

The guards rousted the prisoners from their bunks and marched them upstairs. Berkman recalled, "Helter-skelter the men crowded in, dragging their things with them, badly packed in the haste and confusion." At 4:00 a.m., they were ordered to march. In the frigid air, they trudged across the island that most Americans remember as the first stop for new immigrants. For these prisoners, it was the last stop on their way out.

> *Like shadows we passed through the yard toward the ferry, stumbling on the uneven ground. We did not speak; the prison keepers were also quiet. But the detectives laughed boisterously, and swore and sneered at the silent line. "Don't like this country, damn you! Now you'll get out, ye sons of b———."*
>
> *At last we reached the steamer. I caught sight of three women, our fellow prisoners, being taken aboard. Stealthily, her sirens dumb, the vessel got under way. Within half an hour we boarded the* Buford, *awaiting us in the Bay.*
>
> *At 6 a.m., Sunday, December 21, we started our journey. Slowly the big city receded, wrapped in a milky veil. The tall skyscrapers, their outlines dimmed, looked like fairy tale castles lit by winking stars and then all was swallowed in the distance.*

Berkman was one of 249 foreign-born activists bound for Russia on the USAT *Buford*, which was dubbed "the Soviet Ark" by the press. The onetime cargo ship was being used by the U.S. military as a troop transport and would deposit the men and women in their homeland—"America's Christmas present to Lenin and Trotzky," as the *Literary Digest* put it.

Of the 249 passengers crossing the Atlantic, at least 9 were arrested in Pittsburgh; 13 more hailed from Greensburg, as well as 23 from the Youngstown area and 21 from the northern West Virginia coalfields. Their national origins could be found in their names, likely misspelled by government officials: George Garoshkow, Orteof Sahtabnog, Adolph Schrabel-Delase (or Adolph Schnable), among many others. The accusations varied slightly in many cases. Schnable was arrested in Pittsburgh in February and accused of "advocating or teaching anarchy." Efgram Kovalenko, arrested in Pittsburgh in May, was accused of "[disbelieving] in all organized government." Alexander Antauoff was arrested in Pittsburgh in April for

Adolph Schnable (name spelled various ways), a Russian-born activist with the Union of Russian Workers. Schnable was deported in 1919 on the *Buford*. *Library of Congress.*

"[believing] in the overthrow by force or violence of the government." Many were members of the Union of Russian Workers or of other related groups and anarchist literary circles.

A large proportion of those deported prisoners were from Pittsburgh and its surrounding steel and coal country, which is evidence of the deep roots that radicals had established there. Many of those who were picked up in the region were workers in mines and factories, as Berkman noted in a diary entry several days into his journey:

> *We have organized a committee to assess every "possessing" member of our group for the benefit of the deportees that lack warm clothing. The men from Pittsburgh, Erie and Madison had been shipped to Ellis Island in their working clothes. Many others had also been given no time to take their trunks along. A large pile of the collected apparel—suits, hats, shoes, winter underwear, hosiery, etc.—lies in the center of our cabin, and the*

committee is distributing the things. There is much shouting, laughing and joking. It's our first attempt at practical communism.

Many deportees feared they would be dropped into a region of Russia occupied by the so-called White government that sought to overthrow the Bolsheviks. Others were excited to return home and, in some cases, had hoped to do so for months. Normal travel to Russia was strictly illegal. For most radical immigrants, deportation was the only way to go back to their families. Some vowed to fight for the revolution as soon as they arrived.

The press in Pittsburgh was happy to see them go. A *Pittsburgh Gazette Times* editorial, which was printed several days after the *Buford* left New York, warned of a Soviet plan for American domination. "Since there is no doubt that they seriously propose causing a revolution in this country, it is well that their plans have been revealed in detail….A good beginning has been made in the deportation of 'reds' who were sent hence on the *Buford*," the editor said. "This cleansing work must not be allowed to lag. All aliens who adhere in any degree to anti-government organizations must be sent away and traitorous citizens must be imprisoned."

The USAT *Buford*, an army transport ship that served as the "Soviet Ark" from 1919 to 1920, carrying Russian-born activists to the new Bolshevik state for deportation. *Library of Congress.*

WINTER BRINGS DEFEAT

Winter had hit, and the strikers, both in coal and steel, were approaching their final reserves. The coal miners were now in an illegal "wildcat strike," operating without sanction from their own leaders. Federal agents had targeted the immigrants among them and dragged them away in the dead of night to ship them thousands of miles away. Fuel supplies in many cities were running low, but the federal government wouldn't tolerate much more dissent; President Wilson threatened to send tens of thousands of troops into the mines. A 1919 issue of *Survey* magazine described the situation nationally:

> *In not a few places where temperatures were below zero, a fuel famine existed. In the emergencies much volunteer coal mining was attempted. College and university students went into the surface mines in Kansas. In Montana on the other hand it was reported that Federal troops were used to drive miners to work. The Secretary of War announced that such an action was inconceivable, but there has been no public report on what actually occurred. In North Dakota Governor Frazier took over the mines under martial law and the union miners returned to work under the auspices of the state government.*

By early December, while the Russian arrestees waited in Ellis Island to learn their fate, the mine operators offered a compromise deal: a 14 percent increase. It was far lower than what the miners had demanded, but it was a partial victory, nonetheless. Mine operators coupled the offer with a propaganda campaign nearly identical to the one that the steel trust had used in the Pittsburgh papers: full-page ads, packed with accusations of radicalism and Bolshevism, and atop, a simple message that read, "GO BACK TO THE MINES." Some heeded the call, and more trickled back to work in the weeks to come. In some areas, like Coral, Indiana County, where the police claimed that the Bolsheviks were behind a union-recognition fight, the workers refused to return for months. Running battles would continue for years from Somerset to southern West Virginia, but the great coal strike of 1919 was effectively over.

Attention turned again to the steel mills.

With the end of the coal fight and the ramping up of political repression by the authorities, steel organizers watched their hopes dwindle through December. On December 13, the National Organizing Committee met in

Washington, D.C., where Foster submitted a grim set of statistics. In each strike town, he compared the number of men out of the mills on September 29, which was considered the high point, to the number of those still holding out on December 10. In Pittsburgh, the number of strikers went from 25,000 down to 8,000; in Homestead, that number went from 9,000 to 5,500; and in Braddock and Rankin, that number went from 15,000 to 8,000.

Some districts and mills had dropped precipitously; the Bethlehem Steel plants in eastern Pennsylvania were approaching 100 percent operation. When the strike appeared in Pittsburgh newspapers, it was no longer prominent, and they featured uniformly bad news for the unions. In Wheeling, West Virginia, they reported by mid-December that the strike had collapsed. The meetings of the National Committee only appeared as small wire notes, buried inside the paper. "STEEL STRIKE LEADERS VOTE TO FIGHT ON," noted the *Pittsburgh Press* in three sentences buried among ads for cutlery and dentures. "[A] feeling of pessimism regarding the outcome began to manifest itself among the various international organizations," Foster wrote.

The steel bosses were prepared to declare victory. "The steel strike has been ended for a long time as far as the Steel Corporation is concerned," the *Pittsburgh Post* reported. Judge Elbert Gary of U.S. Steel boasted that the plants were back to 80 percent capacity, and the reduction was due in part to the bosses' refusal to rehire some of the strikers.

Vorse toured an organizing office, where desperate men pleaded with her for evidence that they could still win. "'Ma'am,' he said, 'pretty soon we gotta win, ain't we? Pretty soon we gonna get what we want.' He spoke with intensity, but there was no conviction in his voice. He was pleading with me to reassure him." She assessed the fight:

> *The strike was dying. It was bleeding to death like a living thing. Seep, seep, seep—courage oozed from the men. Seep, seep, seep—they sagged back to work. Each man gutted of his self-respect was a victory for the Steel Companies. Strikes are broken by breaking men's courage; strikes are broken by making men play traitor to what they believe....The strike had not been stamped out. It had not been smothered. But it had been overwhelmed by the great forces against it; it was killed by the indifference of Instituted Labor. So it died, from a slow bleeding. The steel workers' sobbing in the dark hall outside the National Committee Office in Youngstown will always be to me the sound of the dying strike.*

The year 1920 broke with the strike still carrying on. Perhaps one hundred thousand men still held fast across the country, but they represented only a fraction of the total workforce. In the first days of January, strike leaders gathered in Pittsburgh to debate their options. "They were being injured by it far more than was the Steel Trust," Foster recalled. "There was no hope of a settlement, the steel companies being plainly determined to fight on indefinitely."

Indeed, at a Pittsburgh banquet that was held on the same day as the organizers' meeting, Elbert Gary predicted "prosperous times" for America and said wages would eventually have to come down. Gary hailed Pittsburgh's beauty and credited U.S. Steel with the city's prosperity. Nowhere was the strike mentioned. "The officials found plenty of time for mirth and there were many outbursts of gaiety intermingled with business," the *Pittsburgh Gazette Times* reported. "Nirella's orchestra played patriotic and popular music and many times the steel magnates raised their voices in song."

Four days later, on January 8, the union leaders met at the Monongahela House hotel at the corner of Smithfield and today's Fort Pitt Boulevard. In a final vote, they agreed to end the strike and let the men return freely to work—at least those who hadn't been blacklisted. Foster stepped down as secretary-treasurer of the National Committee as a combative, final telegram went out to every striking town and city:

> *The Steel Corporations, with the active assistance of the press, the courts, the federal troops, state police, and many public officials, have denied steel workers their rights of free speech, free assembly and the right to organize, and by this arbitrary and ruthless misuse of power have brought about a condition which has compelled the National Committee for Organizing Iron and Steel Workers to vote today that the active strike phase of the steel campaign is now at an end. A vigorous campaign of education and re-organization will be immediately begun and will not cease until industrial justice has been achieved in the steel industry. All steel strikers are now at liberty to return to work pending preparations for the next big organization movement.*

The Great Steel Strike was over. The commissaries were closed, the plants returned to full capacity and the workers resumed their lives with no tangible victories. The local press treated the strike's end like a foregone conclusion with a handful of smallish articles that focused more on Foster's resignation than on conditions in the mills. Reporters eagerly reminded readers of

Judge Elbert Gary, *left*, with John D. Rockefeller and Calvin Coolidge circa 1925. *Library of Congress.*

Foster's radical background and of his plans for "boring from within" to radicalize the unions. The *Daily Post* noted that the defeated organizer's new replacement had "established a reputation as a foe of the I.W.W." A brief in the *Sunday Morning Post*'s financial section claimed that U.S. Steel's tonnage had already increased by more than one million tons since November. The strike had once covered nine states and hundreds of thousands of workers, as the *Pittsburgh Daily Post* noted, but its end only warranted a few hundred words below the more thrilling stories of the 1920 election and labor strife in the Pittsburgh schools.

Despite all of this, with two phrases—"the active strike phase" and "pending preparations"—the organizers made it clear that they weren't in retreat. When asked for a statement by the *Pittsburgh Daily Post*, Foster replied defiantly, "None of our organizers of the men affected have the slightest feeling of defeat. The campaign has been a success beyond our fondest dreams. The great thing proved is that the iron and steel workers of this country can be organized. It has been done."

In the meantime, new attacks were underway against Pittsburgh's labor radicals. The next battle had already begun.

"THE MOST REVOLUTIONARY PLOT YET UNEARTHED"

The federal agents who infiltrated and rounded up radicals didn't rest on their laurels after their November sweep. They had broken the Union of Russian Workers and deported scores of Pittsburgh-area immigrant radicals, but an atmosphere of hysteria compelled them to go further. Strikes were being broken everywhere, and industrial unions were in retreat; the federal agents had a chance to crush the nation's twin communist parties in their infancy.

Around Pittsburgh, the fledgling parties were small but growing. Industrial workers, especially those from eastern European nations that were convulsed by their own revolutions, were organizing small chapters in steel towns and ethnic neighborhoods. Spies reported that communist leaflets were being circulated at the American Bridge Co. based in Ambridge. Unlike the IWW and fringe groups like the Union of Russian Workers, the Communist Labor Party and the Communist Party of America were tied to a global movement and a foreign government. The parties included many labor organizers and experienced radicals and served as conduits for Russian espionage. John Reed, the famous communist writer and journalist, was reported by Russian authorities as a courier for millions of dollars to the American movement. Although reporters spun exaggerated tales of looted gold that funded Bolshevik plots in America, it was true that the Comintern funded early organizing efforts with smuggled gems and cash.

All of this aroused the interest of the Pittsburgh "Radical Squad" and other federal spies based in the city. One member of the Bureau of Investigation, Henry J. Lenon, was a militant nationalist whose reports were shot through with anti-Semitic language and slurs against non-white activists. Lenon helped direct a small network of spies and informants within the parties; their reports were peppered with suspected communists' names, addresses and roles. Among the purported suspects' names was at least one spy: Louis "Leo" Wendell, who had already infiltrated and influenced the Pittsburgh IWW under his pseudonym, "Walsh."

The authorities planned their strike on the communist parties for January 2, 1920—less than two months after the nationwide raids that sent hundreds of accused Russian anarchists back to their homeland. The *Buford* passengers were still at sea, en route to Finland, when agents under Attorney General Mitchell Palmer launched their second assault.

U.S. attorney general Mitchell Palmer. Palmer spearheaded nationwide raids against left-wing activists and sought to end the 1919 coal strike. *Library of Congress.*

The next day, the *Daily Post* announced, "SIXTY-FIVE TAKEN IN PITTSBURGH RED RAIDS." In raids across Pittsburgh, timed in conjunction with strikes in New York and across the Northeast, police smashed in doors and searched for immigrant communists. At 1207 Fifth Avenue, police struck a building that was "said to be a headquarters" of the Communist Party of America. Under cover of darkness, officers swarmed an office on the third floor. "There, a meeting was discovered in progress, attended by nearly forty men, most of them foreigners," the *Daily Post* reported. "Seven Russians, wanted by the United States government in connection with the condemned organization, were taken into custody." Police claimed to have found Russian-language literature and Communist Party membership cards.

In McKees Rocks, officers swept several suspected communist gathering places and made "a number of arrests," including that of Jacob Balchanas, the Lithuanian-born head of a local communist branch. Other efforts were less impressive. A crew of city detectives struck the Bohemian Hall along Voskamp Street on the North Side, where they "expected to find a number of 'reds' in the hall," the *Daily Post* reported, but when they arrived, they found no reds, no literature and nothing to suggest a communist meeting place. Clearly, the officers claimed, the communists had been tipped off in advance and moved their evidence elsewhere. "In several other places in the Northside district, the detectives [were] met with the same conditions," said the *Post*. A Czechoslovak hall on Nixon Street also contained no communists because the radicals met on Sundays, police explained. Police resorted to raiding individual suspects' empty homes, seizing their left-wing literature and leaving without an arrest. One suspect showed his citizenship papers and was quickly let go, but non-citizen immigrants could be held for lengthy questioning by federal agents, all without legal protections. Reporters detailed the frightening language of the new party's founding documents: "Our organization shall be called the Communist Party of America. Its spirit should be the problems and organization of the laboring classes for

A cartoon representing the Sedition Act of 1918, which enabled a crackdown on left-wing activists. Note the character marked "I.W.W." *Library of Congress.*

the purpose of establishing the dictatorship of the proletariat which will bring about the destruction of the capitalistic class and the realization of the communist society."

The ranks of those arrested swelled in the following days. Ellis Island was packed with foreign-born radicals waiting to be sent home, reports claimed, while Pittsburgh's jails filled with local communists awaiting interrogation. Reports of arrests began to trickle in from outlying towns.

Six men were taken into custody in Vestaburg, a tiny mining hamlet in the Monongahela Valley, and all admitted freely to party membership. Several arrested radicals who lived on the South Side reported that they attended a "School of Bolshevism." These schools dotted Pittsburgh, and reporters warned, "These schools…are being operated on the same order as the public schools." The *Daily Post* said:

> *Small desks are arranged, the walls are covered with blackboards. The lessons in radicalism and anarchy are written upon the blackboards in the various languages of the pupils. Each member is given textbooks and pamphlets to study, and they are urged to promote the work among their friends and even children.*

Perhaps most shocking to Pittsburgh readers was the claim that communists had planned to seize the reins of the steel and coal strikes to spur them into a general revolt. This announcement, which tied the fear of foreign agitators even more closely to ongoing labor battles, was shown prominently in local papers as the twin strikes approached their final days. The *Daily Post* said:

> *Radical leaders planned to develop the recent steel and coal strikes into a general strike and ultimately into a revolution to overthrow the Government, according to information gathered by Federal agents in Friday night's wholesale round up of members of the Communist and Communist Labor parties. A definite program to expand the two labor disturbances for the purpose of blotting out every semblance of organized government was disclosed in evidence gathered in half a score of cities. This data, officials said, tended to prove the nationwide raids had nipped the most menacing revolutionary plot yet unearthed. Officials indicated the radicals were awaiting an opportune moment to carry on among other classes of workers the agitation employed among steel workers and coal miners. Among the foreign element the Communist Party's information described as conclusive revealed the payrolls had been "loaded" with agitators to be sent to every fertile field in support of a general strike.*

Reports described the coal strike committees as being "infested" with communists who urged workers to violence and deterred wavering strikers from going back to the mills and mines. But the mass arrests, scary as they were to everyday readers, didn't end with the destruction of the Pittsburgh communist movement. Hundreds were arrested, but many were soon quietly released. Of the thousands taken in nationwide, only a few hundred would eventually be deported. With the Great War becoming a distant memory and chaos in Europe receding, American politicians were becoming more wary of mass repression, especially after Assistant U.S. Secretary of Labor Louis F. Post dismissed thousands of deportation cases against "alien radicals." Quietly at first, then openly, a movement was building against the Red Scare that had led to so many jail sentences and deportations throughout the steel country. On April 11, 1920, labor leaders and a representative of the newly formed American Civil Liberties Union met at the Labor Lyceum in the Hill District to discuss the ongoing raids. The mass meeting was "part of a nation-wide protest against the continuance of war-time legislation," the *Pittsburgh Daily Post* reported.

LIFE AFTER THE STRIKE

Pittsburgh and the nation settled back into peacetime attitudes in the following months. Strikes continued here and there, but a postwar economic recession deprived industrial workers of the power they had enjoyed when the government protected steel and coal unions. Federal officials slashed the budget that covered espionage against suspected communists and radicals around Pittsburgh, even as the "Radical Squad" expanded its attention beyond Russian-backed militants. As the historian McCormick notes, police investigators began looking into other leftists, as well as black activists, Jewish organizations and Irish immigrant groups tied to the War of Independence that was ravaging their homeland.

The city's communists settled into a new era as well. The parties, now melding into a so-called United Communist Party at the urging of their Russian comrades, were prepared for a twilight existence—partially aboveground and partially organized into clandestine cells. Pittsburgh members, many of whom were born in eastern Europe and spoke English as a second language, still feared deportation. The simple act of distributing labor literature required secret meetups, with papers bundled into cars and hurried off to plants and mills for distribution. H.J. Lenon, the rigidly nationalistic and bigoted special agent tasked with tracking the city's communists, detailed the secrecy and the use of numbered spies in a series of reports from 1920 and 1921. Communist Party members gathered where they thought they might be free from listening ears: a dressing room in an

East Pittsburgh ethnic hall, a member's North Side house, a McKeesport baking company where sympathizers allowed them to store leaflets. Members also worked to organize through ethnic aid societies; a Croatian society with heavy membership in Pittsburgh was allegedly dominated by communists. Still, it took much of the members' time and energy to simply raise enough money for their work. "The Communist Party is in bad FINANCIAL condition," one Pittsburgh spy report acknowledged.

By the time Steve Nelson arrived in Pittsburgh in 1923, there were perhaps two hundred party members in the city. At about twenty years old, the immigrant laborer, born Stjepan Mesaros in rural Croatia, was excited to see the power of the union movement in a great industrial city. The young communist had spent a few years in Philadelphia picking up the language of the radical movement and learning the basics of organizing. He sensed the potential power among radicals in the steel and coal valleys around the city, but Nelson wrote that Pittsburgh itself remained under the sway of the steel bosses and their allies:

It was reasonable to expect Pittsburgh to be a strong labor town, but this was not the case. The steel industry was strictly open shop; any union men were fired and blacklisted, and most other employers followed the example. Workers in the hotel and restaurant and building trades were organized but weak, and the Left was largely ineffective in the city itself.

I bought an old car, and this was requisitioned for the transportation of speakers and literature to the little mining towns along the Allegheny and Monongahela rivers. I listened to the speakers and talked with the miners, many of whom were Croatian immigrants, and what I saw and heard made a deep impression. In the old country families usually sent the biggest son to labor in the Pennsylvania mines, having heard how difficult and dangerous the work was. It was among these single immigrant miners that the Party found its strongest adherents in places like Canonsburg and Uniontown and throughout Washington and Westmoreland counties. Stool pigeons were planted among them, and some men were victimized repeatedly, but it didn't seem to slow them down. The young foreign-born miner didn't own a thing. He put some clothes in a suitcase, stuck the Manifesto in his pocket, changed his name, and moved on to another mining town.

In Pittsburgh, young radicals met at communist halls and debated theory at occasional picnics and social outings. They made contacts at the Heinz plant on the North Side, plastered the Sixteenth Street Bridge (now the David McCullough Bridge) with party flyers and helped start a communist newspaper among Westinghouse workers in Turtle Creek. Electrical factories proved fertile ground for radical organizers, Nelson said, but organizing the steel industry was "a dead letter" since the strike.

William Z. Foster, organizer of the great strike and now a more or less freelance radical unionist, may not have agreed. Foster still maintained his ties to the AFL, but the old radical was quickly drifting toward the communist parties. In 1920, he founded the Trade Union Educational League, which was a group meant to draw labor radicals of all stripes together in the hopes of "boring from within" and seizing control of the old unions. He founded a news magazine, *The Labor Herald*, and a Pittsburgh-based miners' edition, *The Progressive Miner*, which was soon established at the Labor Lyceum at Miller and Reed Streets. The radicals remained on the defensive through the Roaring Twenties, and they circulated their newspapers as they struggled to take control of the unions. Their gathering places remained: the Labor Lyceum on the Hill, the International Socialist Lyceum on the North Side and a collection of party offices and halls scattered in surrounding towns. Through the decade, radicals appeared again in public, and newspaper articles hinted at their survival. A 1927 *Pittsburgh Press* article on a protest meeting presented a list of the activist groups that remained: the South Slavic Workers Club, International Labor Defense and the Socialist Party of Allegheny County. Even the IWW had survived.

In his book on the Great Steel Strike of 1919, Foster himself assessed the movement's victories and defeats—and ended with a call for America's unions to end their internal squabbling and unite against the bosses of every industry. "How long are American progressives going to continue deceiving themselves with the words of high-sounding preambles? When are they going to quit chasing rainbows and settle down to real work?" he wrote. "These are important considerations indeed. The hour when our militants generally adopt English methods, and turn their whole-hearted attention to building up and developing the trade-union movement— that hour will be the dawn of a new day for American Labor."

For the steelworkers and their families, it would be a generation before the seeds planted by the 1919 strike would bear any fruit. The journalist Vorse, while surveying the scene in 1920 after the strike's failure, saw a dark future ahead but hope on the horizon.

Weeks after the strike was over I walked again down Braddock's alleys. The outward flow had set in. Many of my acquaintances had gone back to their own countries....There were no outward changes. The women's curtains were still drying on frames. The children played in the litter. Smoke rolled down the valley. Gusts of white steam arose behind the mill walls.

A woman was sitting beside her door with a child in her arms, another playing at her feet. Her mild eyes gazed on vacancy, as though not seeing the monotony of the squalid street that ended with the red cylinders of the mills, vast structures rearing their monstrous tank-like bulk far into the air and above which rolled the somber magnificence of the smoke. The woman had the patience of eternity in her broad quiet face.

"I have waited," she seemed to say. "I am eternal. This strife is about me and mine. If my brothers do not change this, my sons will. I can wait."

8

EPILOGUE

SMOKY OL' TOWN

The workers held fast outside of the Spang-Chalfant Mill in Ambridge as the deputies advanced. They held clubs and sticks; the deputies, wearing white armbands after a hasty swearing-in by the Beaver County sheriff, carried clubs, shotguns and rifles, and two held Thompson submachine guns menacingly. The sheriff pleaded with the workers to leave their picket; they refused and called him "all kinds of names," as he recounted.

The deputies approached. Shouts were exchanged. Soon, a small group pressed into the strikers. The crowd roared as the deputies swung their clubs into the strikers, who responded in kind. Panicking deputies fired gas canisters into the crowd and surged forward as smoke clouds rolled over the mill town. Before the battle was over, many were injured, and one bystander was dead after being shot in the neck.

Above the mêlée was a banner that read, "Join the Steel and Metal Workers Industrial Union (S.M.W.I.U.)."

It was 1933—fourteen years after the Great Steel Strike of 1919. The Great Depression had rocked the country and afforded labor radicals a new chance to organize both the employed and the masses of unemployed. William Z. Foster, no longer bound to the AFL as its steel organizer, had risen through the ranks of the Communist Party and stood as its presidential candidate in three elections. His grand union organizing project of the 1920s, the Trade Union Educational League, had been transformed into the Trade Union Unity League—a project to form radical "dual unions" that would compete directly with the AFL.

The SMWIU was one such union. Headquartered nationally at Washington Place and Fifth Avenue in Uptown Pittsburgh, the communist-dominated SMWIU represented a new effort to organize steelworkers along vast industrial lines. The Amalgamated had withered to insignificance, but the new radical unions presented an opportunity to finish what it had started. SMWIU organizers fanned out across the steel district, establishing local networks in Ambridge, Coraopolis, McKeesport, McKees Rocks and Homestead, as well as smaller networks in other towns. When members and supporters were arrested in the Ambridge strike, communist-affiliated networks raised funds and organized for their release. Activists organized thousands of unemployed workers in Allegheny County into local councils as part of a nationwide communist project to gain the loyalty of idle laborers.

The SMWIU was far from the only radical union to organize militant actions as the Depression ground on. A year later, in 1934, three violent strikes broke out across the country, each one led by a different radical movement. On the West Coast, longshoremen, organized by communist Australian immigrant "Red" Harry Bridges, shut down ports before police gunfire left several strikers dead. In Minneapolis, Teamsters, led in part by Trotskyist militants, battled police with pipes and clashed with armed strikebreakers. In Ohio, socialist organizers led a strike at the Auto-Lite Spark Plug Works; the strike ended in the bloody "Battle of Toledo," which left two union members dead.

The old union models couldn't hold, and Pittsburgh was a prime example. Even as the Depression ground on, tens of thousands of industrial workers in the steel valleys saw an opportunity to organize as other industries had. Step by step, rank-and-file activists organized their own groups, even as the leaders of the dusty Amalgamated fought them at every turn. When workers planned a meeting in Pittsburgh in January 1935 to discuss a new industry-wide drive, M.F. Tighe, the seventy-six-year-old head of the Amalgamated, branded them as "outlaws." The union's national secretary proclaimed, "This new union talk is a lot of bunk." Lodges that resisted were cast out. A West Virginia worker responded in a letter to the *Pittsburgh Press*, "Now that the bolder lodges have come forward to launch an organizing campaign demanding more aggressive leaders, we are labeled reds and radicals." The battle was no longer between the workers and the bosses—it was between the workers and their own leaders.

Across the country, in several major industries, workers had grown weary of their old leadership. In 1935, several unions joined together to form the

Dues buttons for the Steel Workers Organizing Committee (1937) and the United Steelworkers of America (1942). *Author's collection.*

Committee of Industrial Organization (CIO), a body within the AFL that would push for a new wave of mass organizing in industries like steel. The path that was first laid by William Z. Foster and his allies in Pittsburgh, which many unions followed in order to organize whole industries at once, was now being followed in other fields. The old leaders fought tooth and nail, but the new militant organizers had the edge. In steel, organizers effectively threatened to outflank the Amalgamated leaders unless they joined the new CIO. The union relented, and in June 1936, the rank-and-file members established a new body, which they called the Steel Workers Organizing Committee. The group's founding text bears the "earmarks of one of Labor's historic documents," said the *Pittsburgh Press.* Its national officers worked in the Grant Building downtown.

Much had changed for the workers and the steel bosses. Tough immigration laws passed in the 1920s stemmed the flow of Italian and eastern European laborers. The Depression and the ensuing wave of labor militancy spurred President Franklin D. Roosevelt's administration to pass legislation making it easier than ever for workers to organize. For the first time, companies were barred from forcing workers into no-union "yellow dog" contracts, and the use of company unions was severely curtailed. A congressional committee also revealed the extent of company espionage and police violence used against strikes. The tide was turning toward industry-wide unionization, even as the old guard of the AFL fought against it.

The Red Scare of 1919 was long gone, too. In Washington, Communist Party member Nathan Witt served on the new National Labor Relations Board that oversaw labor disputes (although his party membership would later prompt a political scandal and a purge of the board's radicals). In Pittsburgh, the now-increasingly powerful Communist Party openly operated a book shop on Van Braam Street and a collection of local offices around the city. Tens of thousands of Americans claimed membership. For radical organizers and industrial unionists, victory appeared to be on the horizon.

The industrial union movement's first great victory came as a surprise to business leaders, newspapermen and many unions themselves. On March 2, 1937, the Carnegie-Illinois Steel Co., successor to Carnegie Steel and the main component of the U.S. Steel conglomerate, signed a historic collective bargaining agreement with the now-powerful Steel Workers Organizing Committee. The workers didn't get a closed shop, but they got widespread raises, a forty-hour week with time-and-a-half overtime and a starting wage of five dollars a day for "common labor." The company named for Andrew Carnegie, who had passionately defended the open shop and crushed unions with armed force, now accepted them as equals at the bargaining table. Richard Lamb, a reporter for the *Pittsburgh Press*, reported the shock that day: "Impervious to labor's fifty-year siege, the steel industry's solid front against unions has been smashed with the capitulation of the Carnegie-Illinois Steel Corp. to an 'outside' union's demand for wage conferences," he wrote. "Labor was no less stunned by the series of events leading up to the parleys than independent steel producers and the country at large." The company, the nation's largest steel producer, had long kept an unofficial agreement with the "Little Steel" companies in Johnstown, Youngstown, Chicago and other cities, with unions locked out and wages kept at an even keel. The new deal threatened to upend the entire industry. "Pittsburgh's steel payroll will be increased about twenty-two million dollars annually," the *Press* reported. The effects would be hard to measure, rippling far beyond steel themselves. "Other millions will be added to [the] income of Pittsburghers as industries which normally follow wage changes in the steel industry follow today's raise.…A shortage of skilled labor is expected to develop through Pittsburgh and other steel centers as a result of the adoption of the forty-hour week."

From there, it was only a matter of time before workers in the "Little Steel" companies outside Pittsburgh demanded union deals. The companies balked and prepared for war. A brutal strike broke out weeks after the Carnegie-Illinois deal and lasted for months and left nearly twenty people dead. On Memorial Day 1937 alone, police in Chicago killed ten people and wounded scores more in an attack on strikers. The strike ended in defeat for the unions, but their power grew every year. On November 9, industrial union representatives from across the country gathered at the Islam Grotto on the North Side to formally establish their own alliance and separate from the AFL. Meeting in the arabesque hall under red-white-and blue bunting and a portrait of miners' union head John L. Lewis, the leaders established the Congress of Industrial Organizations.

This surge of industrial unionism at the heart of the steel district even inspired a song from the renowned leftist folk singers Woody Guthrie and Pete Seeger:

> *Pittsburgh town is a smoky ol' town, Pittsburgh*
> *Pittsburgh town is a smoky ol' town, Pittsburgh*
> *Pittsburgh town is a smoky ol' town*
> *Solid iron from McKeesport down*
> *Pittsburgh, Lord God, Pittsburgh*

> *From the Allegheny to the Ohio, in Pittsburgh*
> *Allegheny to the Ohio*
> *Allegheny to the Ohio*
> *They're joining up in the C.I.O.*
> *Pittsburgh, Lord God, Pittsburgh*

The coming war would push workers' power to new heights. The steel makers' profits surged with government contracts as the United States churned out tanks, guns, ships and airplanes. The "Little Steel" companies relented in 1942, when they granted collective deals and guaranteed dues payments to keep the unions' coffers full. Republic Steel, which was a holdout well into the year, eventually folded under a strike threat and the risk of federal action to force its executives' hands. As in World War I, the need for constant production spurred the government to defend steelworkers' efforts. Unlike in World War I, industrial unions had become powerful enough to beat the steel bosses themselves. The Steel Workers Organizing Committee soon became the United Steelworkers of America, with headquarters in Pittsburgh—where it remains today.

One man predicted the great battles and victories of the late 1930s and early 1940s, even as they were just beginning. William Z. Foster, who was then a communist leader in his mid-fifties, published a short book in early 1937, just weeks before U.S. Steel's Carnegie-Illinois division broke the anti-union front that had survived for decades. The book, titled *What Means a Strike in Steel?*, offered lessons from 1919 and from the battles since. Few people had more personal experience.

> *In 1919, after the steel trust, by the use of troops, gunmen, scabs, lying newspapers and mass starvation, had violently broken the strike of 365,000 steel workers and lashed these oppressed toilers back into the mills, I ventured to forecast in my book,* The Great Steel Strike and Its Lessons, *that "it will not be long until they have another big movement under way…the great steel strike of 1919 will seem only a preliminary skirmish when compared with the tremendous battles that are bound to come."*
>
> *This forecast is in all probability about to be realized. Events are fast shaping up for the greatest labor struggle in American history, one that will involve unparalleled masses of striking workers, and probably several industries, in the very heart of the industrial system, with the steel industry as the storm center of the whole movement.*
>
> *When the big steel strike comes, its winning must be made the first order of business for every progressive force in the United States. A great steel strike would be a turning point not only in the trade union movement but in American life generally. The fight of the steel workers for organization is the cutting edge of the struggle of the toiling masses against the whole lineup of reaction and incipient fascism in the United States.*

Foster was imagining the battles on the horizon, not the fight he had lost two decades earlier, but he could easily have described his own strike in the same terms. From the organizers' offices in Pittsburgh to the Monongahela Valley, the outlying towns and across the country, the Great Steel Strike of 1919 opened the road for every victory to come. Its signs linger everywhere, from a shining union headquarters to the rubble of a socialist hall to a parish church in a mill's shadow.

GLOSSARY

AFL: American Federation of Labor, the primary U.S. craft labor organization of the early twentieth century.

AMALGAMATED: Shorthand for Amalgamated Association of Iron and Steel Workers (later Iron, Steel and Tin Workers), the main steel union in the late nineteenth and early twentieth centuries.

ANARCHISM: Political ideology that calls for the destruction of the state and capitalism to be replaced by self-governing communities without hierarchies.

BOLSHEVIK: Faction of Russian socialists (from the Russian word for "majority") who gained power in the October Revolution of 1917. Name used in the United States generically for alleged Soviet sympathizers.

CIO: Congress of Industrial Organizations (and Committee for Industrial Organization), an industrial union movement started in the 1930s.

COMINTERN: International alliance of communist parties established in 1919 and based in Moscow.

COMMUNISM: Political ideology that calls for a workers' movement to overthrow and replace capitalism, with the end goal of a classless and stateless world society. Commonly associated with the Russian model of armed revolution after 1917.

Cossacks: Members of militaristic steppe communities of the former Russian Empire, often employed by the tsars to suppress unrest. Strikers used the term for Pennsylvania state constables and police.

IWW: Industrial Workers of the World, a radical union that called for industrial organizations to overthrow capitalism.

Pinkerton Agency: Private detective agency employed by industrial leaders to spy on labor movements and physically confront strikers and organizers.

SMWIU: Steel and Metal Workers Industrial Union, a short-lived communist-dominated union movement that achieved some success around Pittsburgh in the 1930s.

Socialism: Collection of political ideologies that call for workers' control of society. The term includes both militant revolutionary movements and those that employ gradual political reform.

SWOC: Steel Workers Organizing Committee, a 1930s movement to organize the steel industry.

UMWA: United Mine Workers of America, the primary labor organization representing coal miners.

UORW: Union of Russian Workers (or Union of Russian Workingmen), an immigrant anarchist group targeted by local and federal authorities for deportation.

Wobbly: Self-applied nickname for IWW members. Various stories seek to explain its origin.

Yipsels: Shorthand for members of the Young People's Socialist League or YPSL, the youth wing of the Socialist Party.

BIBLIOGRAPHY

AFL-CIO: America's Unions. "McKees Rocks Strike." www.aflcio.org.

Berkman, Alexander. *The Bolshevik Myth (Diary 1920–1922)*. New York: Boni and Liveright, 1925.

———. *Prison Memoirs of an Anarchist*. New York: Mother Earth Publishing Association, 1912.

Billy Adams Papers, 1911–1942, AIS.1977.26, Archives & Special Collections, University of Pittsburgh Library System.

Brecher, Jeremy. *Strike!* San Francisco: Straight Arrow Books, 1972.

British Pathe. "America. It Happened! (1933)." April 2014. www.youtube.com.

Brody, David. *Labor in Crisis: The Steel Strike of 1919*. Champaign: University of Illinois Press, 1965.

Carnegie, Andrew. "Wealth." *North American Review*, June 1889.

Commission of Inquiry. The Interchurch World Movement. *Report on the Steel Strike of 1919*. New York: Harcourt, Brace and Howe, 1920.

Communist and Anarchist Deportation Cases: Hearings Before a Subcommittee of the Committee on Immigration and Naturalization. House of Representatives, Sixty-Sixth Congress, Second Session, April 21–24, 1920.

Conlin, Joseph H., ed. *At the Point of Production: The Local History of the I.W.W.* Westport, CT: Greenwood Press, 1981.

Davenport, Tim. "Early American Marxism: A Repository of Source Material, 1864–1946." www.marxisthistory.org.

Fitch, John A. *The Steel Workers*. The Pittsburgh Survey. New York: Russell Sage Foundation, 1911.

Foner, Philip S. *Postwar Struggles: 1918–1920*. New York: International Publishers, 1988.

Foster, William Z. *The Great Steel Strike and Its Lessons*. New York: B.W. Huebsch, 1920.

———. *What Means a Strike in Steel?* New York: Workers Library Publishers, 1937.

Heber Blankenhorn Papers, 1919–1937, AIS.1966.15, Archives & Special Collections, University of Pittsburgh Library System.

Hobsbawm, Eric. *The Age of Capital: 1848–1875*. First Vintage Books Edition ed. New York: Vintage Books, 1975.

Holland, W.J. "Eulogy of Andrew Carnegie." Pittsburgh: The Authors Club, 1920.

Howard, Sidney. "The Labor Spy: A Survey of Industrial Espionage." *The New Republic*, 1921.

Hudson, Mark. "The Pittsburgh Reds, 1911–1914: Revolutionary Socialists in Allegheny County." *Against the Current*, July/August 1999.

Indiana (PA) Gazette. Various dates. Newspapers.com.

Investigation of Strike in Steel Industries: Hearing Before the Committee on Education and Labor. United States Senate Sixty-Sixth Congress, First Session, 1919.

Jefferson, Mark. "Our Trade in the Great War." *Geographical Review* 3, no. 6 (1917): 474–80. doi:10.2307/207691.

Johanningsmeier, Edward P. *Forging American Communism: The Life of William Z. Foster*. Princeton, NJ: Princeton University Press, 1994.

Kellogg, Paul U., ed. "The Coal Strike Ended." *The Survey*, December 29, 1919.

Klehr, Harvey, John Earl Haynes and Fridrikh Igorevich Firsov. *The Secret World of American Communism*. New Haven, CT: Yale University Press, 1995.

Mackaman, Thomas. *New Immigrants and the Radicalization of American Labor, 1914–1924*. Jefferson, NC: McFarland & Company, 2017.

Marcus, Dr. Irvin M., Eileen Mountjoy and Beth O'Leary. "The Coal Strike of 1919 in Indiana County and Its Aftermath." IUP Libraries. www.iup.edu.

Marxists Internet Archive. www.marxists.org.

McCollester, Charles. *The Point of Pittsburgh*. Pittsburgh: Battle of Homestead Foundation, 2008.

McCormick, Charles H. *Seeing Reds: Federal Surveillance of the Pittsburgh Mill District, 1917–1921*. Pittsburgh: University of Pittsburgh Press, 1997.

Merrick, Fred. "'Justice' in Pittsburgh." *The International Socialist Review*, September 1911.

Mother Jones. *The Autobiography of Mother Jones*. Chicago: Charles H. Kerr, 1925.

Murray, Robert K. *Red Scare: A Study in National Hysteria, 1919–1920*. Minneapolis: University of Minnesota Press, 1955.

Nasaw, David. *Andrew Carnegie*. New York: Penguin Books, 2007.

Nelson, Steve, James R. Barrett and Rob Ruck. *Steve Nelson: American Radical*. Pittsburgh: University of Pittsburgh Press, 1981.

New Castle (PA) News. Various dates. Newspapers.com.

Newsinger, John. *Fighting Back: The American Working Class in the 1930s*. London: Bookmarks Publications, 2012.

Perelman, Dale Richard. *Road to Rust: The Disintegration of the Steel Industry in Western Pennsylvania and Eastern Ohio*. Charleston, SC: The History Press, 2018.

———. *Steel: The Story of Pittsburgh's Iron & Steel Industry, 1852–1902*. Charleston, SC: The History Press, 2014.

Pittsburgh Daily Post. Various dates. Newspapers.com.

Pittsburgh Gazette Times. Various dates. Newspapers.com.

Pittsburgh Press. Various dates. Newspapers.com.

Serrin, William. *Homestead: The Glory and Tragedy of an American Steel Town*. New York: Times Books, 1992.

Standiford, Les. *Meet You in Hell: Andrew Carnegie, Henry Clay Frick, and the Bitter Partnership That Transformed America*. New York: Three Rivers Press, 2005.

Trautmann, William. *Riot*. Chicago: Chicago Labor Printing Company, 1922.

University of Pittsburgh. "Pittsburgh and Western Pennsylvania Labor Legacy." www.exhibit.library.pitt.edu.

Vorse, Mary Heaton. *Men and Steel*. New York: Boni and Liveright, 1920.

West Virginian (Fairmont, WV). Various dates. Newspapers.com.

INDEX

ABOUT THE AUTHOR

Ryan C. Brown is a journalist and writer based in Pittsburgh. Born in Pittsburgh and raised nearby, Ryan studied journalism at the University of Pittsburgh at Johnstown and has covered politics, local government and history for several western Pennsylvania news outlets. Along with his wife, Kelly, he is active in the labor movement and in community organizations.